EDITOR-IN-CHIEF: Mary Coleman

FOOD EDITOR: Pamela Clark

● ● ●

ART DIRECTOR: Sue de Guingand

ARTIST: Annemarlene Hissink

● ● ●

ASSISTANT FOOD EDITORS: Kathy McGarry, Louise Patniotis

ASSOCIATE FOOD EDITORS: Karen Hammial, Lucy Kelly

SENIOR HOME ECONOMIST: Justin Kerr

HOME ECONOMISTS: Emma Braz, Nadia Kretchmer, Maria Sampsonis, Jodie Tilse, Amal Webster, Lovoni Welch

EDITORIAL COORDINATOR: Elizabeth Hooper

KITCHEN ASSISTANT: Amy Wong

STYLISTS: Carolyn Fienberg, Kay Francis, Jane Hann, Cherise Koch, Sophia Young

PHOTOGRAPHERS: Robert Clark, Robert Taylor

● ● ●

HOME LIBRARY STAFF

ASSISTANT EDITORS:
Mary-Anne Danaher, Lynne Testoni

EDITORIAL COORDINATOR: Lee Stephenson

● ● ●

CIRCULATION & MARKETING DIRECTOR:
Chris Gibson

PUBLISHER/MANAGING DIRECTOR: Colin Morrison

CHIEF EXECUTIVE OFFICER: Richard Walsh

● ● ●

Produced by The Australian Women's Weekly Home Library.
Colour separations by ACP Colour Graphics Pty Ltd., Sydney.
Printing by Hannanprint, Sydney.
Published by ACP Publishing Pty. Limited,
54 Park Street, Sydney.
◆ AUSTRALIA: Distributed by Network Distribution
Company, 54 Park Street Sydney, (02) 9282 8777.
◆ UNITED KINGDOM: Distributed in the U.K. by Australian
Consolidated Press (UK) Ltd, 20 Galowhill Rd, Brackmills,
Northampton NN4 7EE (01604) 760 456.
◆ CANADA: Distributed in Canada by Whitecap Books Ltd,
351 Lynn Ave, North Vancouver B.C. V7J 2C4 (604) 980 9852.
◆ NEW ZEALAND: Distributed in New Zealand by Netlink
Distribution Company, 17B Hargreaves St, Level 5,
College Hill, Auckland 1 (9) 302 7616.
◆ SOUTH AFRICA: Distributed in South Africa by Intermag,
PO Box 57394, Springfield 2137, Johannesburg (011) 491 7534.

● ● ●

Easy Spanish-style Cookery

Includes index.
ISBN 1 86396 054 6

1. Cookery, Spanish. I. Title: Australian
Women's Weekly. (Series: Australian
Women's Weekly Home Library).

641.5946

● ● ●

© A C P Publishing Pty. Limited 1997
ACN 053 273 546
◆ This publication is copyright. No part of it may be
reproduced or transmitted in any form without the
written permission of the publishers.

● ● ●

COVER: Clockwise from back: Scalloped Potato and Leek
Casserole, page 101; Stuffed Red and Yellow Peppers, page 86;
Seafood Casserole, page 64. *Tiles from Country Floors.*
OPPOSITE: Gazpacho, page 53.
Pepper grinder and wire basket from Accoutrement.
BACK COVER: Catalan Cinnamon Custard, page 114.
*Rug and sunflower plate from Sirocco Homewares;
spoon from Kitchen Kapers.*

● ● ●

Easy Spanish-style cookery

This delectable collection introduces one of Europe's most flavoursome, least-known styles of cooking into your repertoire of favourite recipes. Too often confused with Mexican food, Spanish cooking bears more resemblance to the cuisines of France and Italy with its robust, exciting tastes. All these ingredients are available from supermarkets and good greengrocers, and there is a glossary explaining unusual names and cooking terms. The detailed step-by-step photography and glorious pictures of the finished dishes will both inspire and assist you in presenting an authentic Spanish meal.

Pamela Clark

FOOD EDITOR

BRITISH & NORTH AMERICAN READERS: Please note that Australian cup and spoon measurements are metric. A quick conversion guide appears on page 127.
A glossary explaining unfamiliar terms and ingredients appears on page 122.

TAPAS

Translated as "lid", satisfying tapas put a lid on the Spaniards' hunger, eaten before their late lunch and even later dinner with a glass of sherry. Make a half-dozen or so of the recipes in this chapter and pass them to guests with drinks before dinner or, even better, as an authentically Spanish entree.

CHORIZO PUFFS

1/4 cup (60ml) olive oil
1 (170g) chorizo sausage,
    finely chopped
1 small (150g) red pepper,
    finely chopped
1 cup (150g) self-raising flour
1/3 cup (55g) cornmeal
3 cloves garlic, crushed
3 eggs, separated
3/4 cup (180ml) beer
1 cup (100g) grated
    manchego cheese
1/4 cup chopped fresh parsley
vegetable oil, for deep-frying

2. Combine sifted flour and cornmeal in medium bowl, gradually whisk in remaining olive oil, garlic, egg yolks and beer. Cover, stand 30 minutes.

4. Deep-fry level tablespoons of puff mixture in hot oil, in batches, until just browned and cooked through; drain on absorbent paper.

Makes about 40.

■ Best made just before serving.
■ Freeze: Not suitable.
■ Microwave: Not suitable.

1. Heat 2 teaspoons of the olive oil in medium pan, cook sausage and pepper, stirring, until sausage is well browned; drain on absorbent paper.

3. Stir sausage mixture, manchego and parsley into batter. Beat egg whites in small bowl with electric mixer until soft peaks form; fold into batter in 2 batches.

ORANGE-GLAZED CALAMARI

750g small calamari hoods
3 cloves garlic, crushed
1 teaspoon ground sweet paprika
2 teaspoons grated orange rind
1 tablespoon orange juice
1 tablespoon red wine vinegar
¼ cup (50g) brown sugar
1 tablespoon olive oil
1 tablespoon chopped fresh
   coriander leaves

1. Cut calamari hoods open, score shallow diagonal slashes across inside surface. Cut into 2cm x 5cm pieces.

2. Combine calamari, garlic, paprika, rind, juice, vinegar, sugar and oil in medium bowl. Cover, refrigerate for 3 hours or overnight. Drain calamari over bowl; reserve marinade.

3. Cook calamari, in greased heated griddle pan (or grill or barbecue), in batches, until pieces start to curl and are almost cooked. Add reserved marinade to pan, simmer, uncovered, about 1 minute or until slightly thickened. Combine calamari and marinade mixture with coriander in bowl.

Serves 6 to 8.

▨ Can be prepared a day ahead.
▨ Storage: Covered, in refrigerator.
▨ Freeze: Not suitable.
▨ Microwave: Not suitable.

Pots from Brazil Galleria

DEEP-FRIED OYSTERS WITH CHILLI DRESSING

24 oysters on half shells
1/3 cup (55g) cornmeal
vegetable oil, for deep-frying

CHILLI DRESSING
2 tablespoons white wine vinegar
1/4 cup (60ml) olive oil
2 small fresh red chillies,
   finely chopped
1/2 teaspoon sugar
1 tablespoon chopped fresh parsley

1. Remove oysters from shells. Wash shells, place on oven tray, heat in slow oven 10 minutes.

2. Toss oysters in cornmeal then deep-fry in hot oil, in batches, until lightly browned; drain on absorbent paper. Serve oysters in hot shells, drizzle with Chilli Dressing.
Chilli Dressing: Combine all ingredients in jar; shake well.

Serves 4 to 6.

■ Oysters must be made just before serving. Chilli Dressing can be made 3 days ahead.
■ Storage: Dressing, covered, in refrigerator.
■ Freeze: Not suitable.
■ Microwave: Not suitable.

SAFFRON PRAWNS WITH ROMESCO SAUCE

1.2kg uncooked large prawns
½ cup (75g) plain flour
½ cup (125ml) beer
1½ tablespoons olive oil
pinch saffron powder
2 egg whites
vegetable oil, for deep-frying

ROMESCO SAUCE
1 small (150g) red pepper
2 small (260g) tomatoes, halved
4 cloves garlic, unpeeled
1 tablespoon olive oil
1 slice white bread, chopped
¼ cup (40g) blanched almonds
1 small (80g) onion, chopped
1 small fresh red chilli, chopped
1 teaspoon ground sweet paprika
2 tablespoons red wine vinegar
1 tablespoon water
1½ teaspoons sugar
⅓ cup (80ml) olive oil, extra

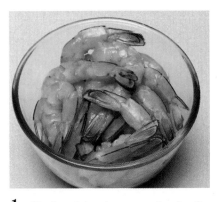

1. Shell and devein prawns, leaving the tails intact.

2. Sift flour into medium bowl, gradually whisk in combined beer, oil and saffron until smooth. Cover, stand 30 minutes. Beat egg whites in small bowl until soft peaks form, fold into batter.

3. Dip prawns in batter, drain off excess. Deep-fry prawns in hot oil, in batches, until lightly browned and cooked through; drain on absorbent paper. Serve with Romesco Sauce.

4. Romesco Sauce: Halve pepper lengthways, remove seeds and membranes. Place pepper, tomatoes and garlic in small greased baking dish, bake in hot oven about 25 minutes or until pepper is soft. Cover vegetables with baking paper for 5 minutes then peel away skins.

5. Heat oil in medium pan, cook bread and nuts, stirring about 2 minutes or until browned; drain on absorbent paper. Add onion, chilli and paprika to same pan, cook, stirring, until onion is soft.

6. Process pepper, tomatoes, garlic, bread mixture, onion mixture, vinegar, water and sugar until smooth. With motor operating, add extra oil gradually, in thin stream; process until combined.

Serves 6 to 8.

■ Prawns best made just before serving. Romesco Sauce can be made a day ahead.
■ Storage: Covered, in refrigerator.
■ Freeze: Not suitable.
■ Microwave: Not suitable.

GARLIC WINE CLAMS WITH CHOPPED TOMATOES

2kg clams
3 teaspoons coarse cooking salt
1/4 cup (60ml) olive oil
3 cloves garlic, chopped
2/3 cup fresh parsley sprigs,
**   loosely packed**
1/2 cup (125ml) lemon juice
1 medium (150g) onion,
**   finely chopped**
3/4 cup (180ml) dry white wine
4 small (520g) tomatoes, quartered,
**   seeded, chopped**

1. Rinse clams under cold water; place in large bowl, sprinkle with salt, cover with cold water. Soak 1½ hours. Discard water; rinse and drain clams.

2. Blend or process oil, garlic, parsley and juice until well combined.

3. Heat oil mixture in large pan; cook onion, stirring, until soft. Add clams and wine; cook, covered, stirring occasionally, about 8 minutes or until clams open (discard any unopened clams). Remove clams with slotted spoon to large bowl; reserve half cup (125ml) cooking liquid, discard the remaining liquid. Combine reserved liquid and tomatoes, pour over clams to serve.

Serves 6 to 8.

■ Best made just before serving.
■ Freeze: Not suitable.
■ Microwave: Not suitable.

MARINATED OLIVES

Chilli Olives

500g black olives
5 small fresh red chillies, chopped
3 cloves garlic, crushed
1 teaspoon ground cumin
1 teaspoon chilli powder
**1/2 small (75g) red pepper,
   finely chopped**
2 green onions, finely chopped
2 tablespoons lemon juice
2 tablespoons red wine vinegar
1/3 cup (80ml) olive oil

1. Combine all ingredients in medium bowl. Cover, refrigerate at least 2 days before serving.

Citrus Herb Olives

250g black olives
250g green olives
2 teaspoons grated lemon rind
2 teaspoons grated orange rind
2 teaspoons fennel seeds, toasted
2 teaspoons cumin seeds, toasted
1/4 teaspoon ground cinnamon
1 small (80g) onion, finely chopped
2 tablespoons lemon juice
1/4 cup (60ml) white wine vinegar
1/3 cup (80ml) olive oil
**2 tablespoons shredded fresh
   mint leaves**

1. Combine all ingredients in medium bowl. Cover, refrigerate at least 2 days before serving.

Makes about 3 cups olives.

■ Can be made a week ahead.
■ Storage: Covered, separately, in refrigerator.
■ Freeze: Not suitable.
■ Microwave: Not suitable.

Plate and small dish from Corso De' Fiori

SPANISH POTATO OMELETTE

5 large (1.5kg) potatoes
1 medium (150g) onion, thinly sliced
olive oil, for shallow-frying
8 eggs, lightly beaten
1 teaspoon ground sweet paprika
¼ cup (60ml) olive oil, extra

1. Peel and cut potatoes into very thin slices, pat dry with absorbent paper. Shallow-fry potatoes and onion in hot oil, in batches, until just soft, but not browned. Transfer potatoes and onion to strainer; cool.

2. Place strained potatoes and onion in large bowl, add combined eggs and paprika; stand 5 minutes.

3. Heat extra oil in 26cm non-stick pan. Pour in potato mixture, press down firmly. Cook, uncovered, over low heat, about 15 minutes or until potatoes are soft and base of omelette is browned.

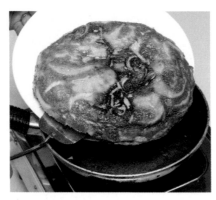

4. Carefully invert potato omelette onto large plate; slide back into same pan. Cook, uncovered, over low heat, for about 10 minutes or until base is browned and omelette set. Stand for 10 minutes, before cutting into wedges.

Serves 6 to 8.

■ Best made just before serving.
■ Freeze: Not suitable.
■ Microwave: Not suitable.

Bowl and plate from Corso De' Fiori

CHILLI GARLIC MUSHROOMS

⅓ cup (80ml) olive oil
50g butter
6 cloves garlic, crushed
2 small fresh red chillies,
    finely chopped
1kg button mushrooms
1 tablespoon lemon juice
½ teaspoon cracked black pepper
2 tablespoons chopped
    fresh parsley

Serves 6 to 8.
■ Best made just before serving.
■ Freeze: Not suitable.
■ Microwave: Not suitable.

1. Heat oil and butter in large pan, add garlic, chillies and mushrooms, cook, stirring, about 5 minutes or until mushrooms are tender. Add remaining ingredients.

HERBED OLIVE AND ANCHOVY DIP

8 anchovy fillets in oil, drained
¼ cup (60ml) milk
2 tablespoons olive oil
1 slice white bread, chopped
1 small (100g) red onion, chopped
1 clove garlic, crushed
2 tablespoons chopped
fresh parsley
2 teaspoons chopped fresh
marjoram leaves
1 teaspoon chopped fresh
thyme leaves
¼ cup (30g) seeded black
olives, chopped
1½ tablespoons drained capers,
rinsed, chopped
2 teaspoons red wine vinegar
1 tablespoon lemon juice
2 tablespoons olive oil, extra

1. Combine anchovies and milk in small bowl, stand 10 minutes; drain well.

2. Heat half the oil in medium pan, add bread, cook, stirring, until lightly browned; remove from pan. Heat remaining oil in same pan, cook onion, garlic and herbs, stirring, until onion is soft.

3. Process anchovies, bread, onion mixture, olives, capers, vinegar and juice until combined. Add extra oil while motor is operating; process mixture until almost smooth.

Makes about 1 cup (250ml).

■ Best made a day ahead.
■ Storage: Covered, in refrigerator.
■ Freeze: Not suitable.
■ Microwave: Not suitable.

GOATS' CHEESE WITH CHILLI AND TARRAGON

500g firm goats' cheese
1½ cups (375ml) olive oil
2 tablespoons red wine vinegar
**2 tablespoons chopped fresh
    tarragon leaves**
**2 small fresh red chillies,
    finely chopped**
6 cloves garlic, crushed
½ teaspoon cracked black pepper

Makes about 2½ cups.
■ Can be prepared 4 days ahead.
■ Storage: Covered, in refrigerator.
■ Freeze: Not suitable.
■ Microwave: Not suitable.

1. Cut cheese into 3cm cubes, combine with remaining ingredients in large bowl; cover, refrigerate overnight. Drain cheese mixture over bowl, reserving 2 tablespoons of the oil mixture to drizzle over cheese just before serving.

PRAWNS WITH GARLIC HERB BUTTER

1kg uncooked medium prawns
2 tablespoons olive oil
6 cloves garlic, crushed
50g butter, chopped
1 tablespoon lemon juice
1½ tablespoons chopped
fresh parsley

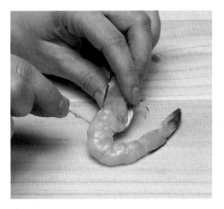

1. Shell and devein prawns, leaving heads and tails intact.

2. Heat oil in large pan, cook garlic, stirring, until soft. Add prawns to pan, cook, turning gently, until prawns start to change colour and are almost cooked. Add butter and juice, cook, until prawns are just cooked through. Stir in parsley.

Serves 6 to 8.

■ Best made just before serving.
■ Freeze: Not suitable.
■ Microwave: Not suitable.

Tiles from Country Floors

MINI PIZZAS WITH RED PEPPER PASTE

3 cups (450g) plain flour
2 teaspoons dry yeast
2 teaspoons sugar
1 teaspoon coarse cooking salt
1¼ cups (310ml) water
1 tablespoon olive oil
1 medium (170g) red onion,
**   thinly sliced**
1 cup (120g) seeded black
**   olives, sliced**
½ cup (125ml) olive oil, extra
¼ cup chopped fresh parsley

RED PEPPER PASTE
3 medium (600g) red peppers
4 cloves garlic, crushed
½ teaspoon cayenne pepper
1 tablespoon red wine vinegar
2 tablespoons olive oil

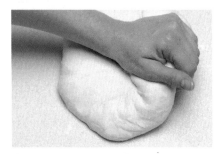

1. Sift flour into large bowl, add yeast, sugar, salt, water and oil; mix to a soft dough. Knead on floured surface about 5 minutes or until smooth and elastic.

2. Place dough in large greased bowl; cover, stand in warm place for about 30 minutes or until doubled in size.

3. Turn dough onto floured surface, knead until smooth. Divide dough into 20 pieces; roll each out into 8cm rounds.

4. Place rounds on greased oven trays. Leaving a 1cm border, spread rounds with Red Pepper Paste, top with onion and olive slices. Brush edges of Pizzas with a little of the extra oil. Bake in moderately hot oven about 15 minutes or until just browned and cooked. Sprinkle parsley over Pizzas; drizzle with remaining extra oil.

5. Red Pepper Paste: Quarter peppers, remove seeds and membranes. Roast under grill or in very hot oven, skin side up, until skin blisters and blackens. Cover pepper pieces in plastic or paper for 5 minutes, then peel away skin; roughly chop peppers. Blend or process peppers with remaining ingredients until almost smooth.

Makes 20.

■ Red Pepper Paste can be made a day ahead.
■ Storage: Covered, in refrigerator.
■ Freeze: Not suitable.
■ Microwave: Not suitable.

Tray and jug from Corso De' Fiori; glass and coir mat from Freedom Furniture

SPICY PORK SKEWERS

Soak bamboo skewers in water 3 hours or overnight to prevent them burning.

750g pork fillets
6 cloves garlic, crushed
1 tablespoon ground cumin
2 teaspoons ground coriander
2 teaspoons ground hot paprika
¼ cup chopped fresh parsley
2 tablespoons chopped fresh oregano leaves
½ cup (125ml) olive oil

1. Cut pork into 3cm cubes, combine with remaining ingredients in large bowl. Cover; refrigerate 3 hours or overnight.

2. Thread pork onto skewers; discard remaining spice mixture.

3. Cook skewers, in batches, in greased heated griddle pan (or grill or barbecue) until browned and cooked through.

Makes 12.

▨ Can be made a day ahead.
▨ Storage: Covered, in refrigerator.
▨ Freeze: Uncooked skewers suitable.
▨ Microwave: Not suitable.

SALT COD WITH CHILLI AND TOMATOES

450g salt cod
1 large (300g) red onion
1 tablespoon olive oil
2 cloves garlic, sliced
1 small fresh red chilli, sliced
4 medium (760g) tomatoes, peeled, chopped
½ cup (60g) seeded black olives
¼ cup (60ml) tomato paste
¼ cup (60ml) dry white wine
1 tablespoon lemon juice
1 tablespoon drained capers, rinsed, chopped
3 teaspoons sugar
¼ cup chopped fresh parsley

1. Place cod in large bowl, cover with cold water. Cover bowl with plastic wrap, refrigerate 24 hours, changing water several times. Drain cod, add to large pan of boiling water, simmer, uncovered, 1 minute. Drain, rinse under cold water; drain well.

2. Flake cod using fork; discard skin and bones.

3. Cut onion into wedges. Heat oil in large pan, cook onion, garlic and chilli, stirring, until onion is almost soft. Add tomatoes, olives, paste, wine, juice, capers and sugar. Simmer, covered, 5 minutes, then simmer uncovered another 5 minutes or until slightly thickened. Stir in cod and parsley.

Serves 6 to 8.

■ Best made just before serving. Salt cod must be prepared 24 hours ahead. Sauce can be prepared the day before.
■ Storage: Covered, separately, in refrigerator.
■ Freeze: Not suitable.
■ Microwave: Not suitable.

SNAILS IN GREEN SAUCE

You will need the snail's shells for this recipe.

1 tablespoon olive oil
1 small (80g) onion, finely chopped
4 cloves garlic, crushed
1 teaspoon plain flour
2 tablespoons dry white wine
1/4 cup (60ml) fish stock
2 tablespoons cream
1/4 cup chopped fresh parsley
24 large canned snails, drained
rock salt

2. Gradually stir in combined wine, stock and cream; stir over heat until sauce boils and thickens. Stir in parsley.

3. Push the snails into shells; spoon sauce into shells. Arrange shells on rock salt, in shallow ovenproof dish. Bake, uncovered, in hot oven for about 5 minutes or until heated through.

Serves 4 to 6.

■ Best made just before serving.
■ Freeze: Not suitable.
■ Microwave: Suitable.

1. Heat oil in small pan; cook onion and garlic, stirring, until onion is soft. Add flour, stir over heat until bubbling.

ROASTED SPICY RED PEPPERS

6 medium (1.2kg) red peppers
2 tablespoons red wine vinegar
¼ cup (60ml) olive oil
2 cloves garlic, crushed
¼ teaspoon cayenne pepper
fresh marjoram leaves

1. Quarter peppers, remove seeds and membranes. Roast peppers in baking dish, uncovered, in moderately hot oven about 45 minutes, turning occasionally, until skin blisters and blackens. Remove from pan, cover pepper pieces with plastic or paper for 5 minutes, peel away skin.

2. Stir vinegar, oil and garlic into pan juices in baking dish; cook, stirring, until garlic is just soft; strain into jug. Place peppers, in single layer, in serving dish; pour oil mixture over top, sprinkle with cayenne pepper. Cover, refrigerate for 3 hours or overnight. Serve sprinkled with marjoram.

Makes about 5 cups.

- Can be made 3 days ahead.
- Storage: Covered, in refrigerator.
- Freeze: Not suitable.
- Microwave: Not suitable.

Handpainted ceramics from Anna Paola Frame, Sydney.

LAMB AND CHORIZO EMPANADILLAS

2 cups (300g) plain flour
1/4 cup (60ml) olive oil
2 teaspoons lemon juice
2/3 cup (160ml) milk, approximately
1 egg, lightly beaten

FILLING
2 teaspoons olive oil
1 small (80g) onion, finely chopped
2 cloves garlic, crushed
150g minced lamb
1/2 (85g) chorizo sausage, finely chopped
2 tablespoons tomato paste
2 tablespoons dry red wine
1 tablespoon seeded black olives, chopped
1/4 cup (60ml) chicken stock

1. Sift flour into large bowl; add oil, juice and just enough milk to make a soft dough.

2. Knead dough on floured surface until smooth. Cover with plastic wrap, stand 10 minutes.

3. Divide dough in half; roll each half between sheets of baking or grease-proof paper until 2mm thick; cut each into 12 x 8.5cm rounds.

4. Place rounded teaspoons of filling in centre of each round; fold over, pinch edges firmly together to seal. Place Empanadillas on greased oven trays, brush with egg. Bake in moderately hot oven about 15 minutes or until browned.

5. Filling: Heat oil in medium pan, cook onion and garlic, stirring, until onion is soft. Add lamb, cook, stirring, until well browned. Add the remaining ingredients, simmer, uncovered, about 5 minutes or until thickened slightly; cool.

Makes about 24.

■ Filling can be made a day ahead.
■ Storage: Covered, in refrigerator.
■ Freeze: Uncooked Empanadillas suitable.
■ Microwave: Not suitable.

Plate from Corso De' Fiori

FRIED CHORIZO WITH GARLIC

4 (680g) chorizo sausages
2 tablespoons olive oil
2 cloves garlic, crushed
½ cup chopped fresh parsley

1. Cut sausages into 5mm slices.

2. Add sausage slices to large heated pan, cook, stirring, until crisp; drain on absorbent paper. Discard fat.

3. Heat oil in same pan, add sausage slices, garlic and parsley, stir until just heated through.

Serves 6 to 8.

■ Best made just before serving.
■ Freeze: Not suitable.
■ Microwave: Not suitable.

Tiles from Country Floors; plate from Orson & Blake Collectables; pot from Brazil Galleria

Plate from The Bay Tree Kitchen Shop

ZUCCHINI WITH CHILLI BASIL DRESSING

6 medium (720g) zucchini
⅓ cup (80ml) olive oil
2 tablespoons red wine vinegar
2 tablespoons chopped fresh
   basil leaves
2 small fresh red chillies, chopped

Serves 4 to 6.
■ Can be made a day ahead.
■ Storage: Covered, in refrigerator.
■ Freeze: Not suitable.
■ Microwave: Not suitable.

1. Cut zucchini lengthways into 5mm slices; cook on both sides, in batches, in greased heated griddle pan (or grill or barbecue) until charred and tender. Combine hot zucchini with remaining ingredients in large bowl; cover, stand at room temperature for at least 1 hour before serving.

POTATOES WITH GARLIC MAYONNAISE

40 (1.6kg) tiny potatoes, halved
1 tablespoon chopped fresh parsley
¼ teaspoon cayenne pepper

GARLIC MAYONNAISE
1 medium (70g) bulb garlic
2 teaspoons light olive oil
2 egg yolks
1 tablespoon lemon juice
1 cup (250ml) light olive oil, extra
1 tablespoon hot water,
  approximately

2. **Garlic Mayonnaise:** Put unpeeled garlic bulb on oven tray, brush with oil. Bake garlic, uncovered, in moderately hot oven, about 45 minutes or until soft; cool 15 minutes. Cut garlic in half cross-ways; squeeze pulp from cloves.

1. Boil, steam or microwave potatoes until tender. Drain potatoes, cool. Gently mix potatoes, Garlic Mayonnaise and parsley in large bowl. Cover, refrigerate 3 hours or overnight; sprinkle with cayenne pepper.

3. Blend or process garlic pulp with egg yolks and juice until smooth. Add extra oil, gradually, in a thin stream while motor is operating; add enough water to make a pouring consistency.

Serves 8 to 10.

▓ Can be made a day ahead.
▓ Storage: Covered, in refrigerator.
▓ Freeze: Not suitable.
▓ Microwave: Potatoes suitable.

Bowl from Mexico

CHAR-GRILLED CHILLI OCTOPUS

1kg baby octopus
¼ cup (60ml) olive oil
⅓ cup (80ml) lemon juice
6 cloves garlic, crushed
4 small fresh red chillies,
**   finely chopped**
1 tablespoon ground sweet paprika

1. Remove and discard heads and beaks from octopus, cut in half.

2. Combine octopus with remaining ingredients in medium bowl; cover, refrigerate 3 hours or overnight.

3. Char-grill octopus, in greased heated griddle pan (or grill or barbecue), in batches, until tender.

Serves 6 to 8.

- Can be prepared a day ahead.
- Storage: Covered, in refrigerator.
- Freeze: Not suitable.
- Microwave: Not suitable.

BRAISED MEATBALLS WITH GREEN OLIVES

1kg minced pork and veal
3 cloves garlic, crushed
1 tablespoon chopped fresh
**   oregano leaves**
2 tablespoons chopped
**   fresh parsley**
1 cup (70g) stale breadcrumbs
1 egg, lightly beaten
2 tablespoons olive oil
1 large (200g) onion, finely chopped
1 teaspoon ground sweet paprika
2 small fresh red chillies, chopped
1 cinnamon stick
2 x 425g cans tomatoes
1 cup (250ml) beef stock
2 tablespoons tomato paste
2 cups (240g) seeded green olives

1. Combine mince, garlic, herbs, breadcrumbs and egg in medium bowl. Roll level tablespoons of mixture into balls. Place on tray in single layer; cover, refrigerate 30 minutes.

2. Heat half the oil in large pan; cook meatballs, in batches, until browned. Drain on absorbent paper.

3. Heat remaining oil in same pan; cook onion, paprika and chillies, stirring, until onion is soft. Add cinnamon, undrained crushed tomatoes, stock and paste; simmer, uncovered, about 10 minutes or until sauce starts to thicken. Add meatballs and olives; simmer, uncovered, about 10 minutes or until meatballs are cooked through and sauce has thickened. Discard cinnamon stick.

Makes about 50.

▨ Can be made a day ahead.
▨ Storage: Covered, in refrigerator.
▨ Freeze: Suitable.
▨ Microwave: Not suitable.

CRISPY MARINATED WHITEBAIT

1kg fresh or frozen whitebait
½ cup (125ml) red wine vinegar
4 cloves garlic, crushed
2 tablespoons chopped fresh
**   oregano leaves**
1 small fresh red chilli,
**   finely chopped**
1 teaspoon cracked black pepper
½ cup (75g) plain flour
vegetable oil, for deep-frying

1. Combine whitebait, vinegar, garlic, oregano, chilli and pepper in large bowl; cover, refrigerate 3 hours or overnight.

2. Drain the whitebait, pat dry with absorbent paper.

3. Toss flour and whitebait together in large bowl.

4. Deep-fry whitebait in hot oil, in batches, until lightly browned. Drain on absorbent paper.

Serves 6 to 8.

▨ Best made just before serving.
▨ Freeze: Not suitable.
▨ Microwave: Not suitable.

Pewter and ceramic plate and spoon from Corso De' Fiori; coir mat from Freedom Furniture

PAELLA CROQUETTES

You will need to cook 1 cup (200g) calrose rice for this recipe.

2 tablespoons olive oil
1 large (200g) onion,
   roughly chopped
4 cloves garlic, crushed
1 teaspoon ground sweet paprika
200g scallops
750g medium uncooked prawns,
   shelled
120g piece boneless white fish,
   skinned, chopped
¼ cup fresh parsley sprigs,
   loosely packed
3 cups cooked calrose rice
4 eggs
¾ cup (90g) frozen peas
plain flour
1 cup (100g) dried breadcrumbs
vegetable oil, for deep-frying

1. Heat oil in small pan, cook onion, garlic and paprika; stirring, until onion is soft.

2. Process onion mixture, seafood and parsley until smooth. Combine seafood mixture, rice, 1 of the eggs and peas in large bowl.

3. Shape quarter cups of mixture into 12cm logs, roll gently in flour, dip in remaining beaten eggs, then crumbs. Place in single layer on tray, cover with plastic wrap, refrigerate 1 hour. Deep-fry Croquettes in hot oil, in batches, until browned; drain on absorbent paper. Serve immediately.

Makes about 18.

- Can be prepared a day ahead.
- Storage: Covered, in refrigerator.
- Freeze: Uncooked crumbed Croquettes suitable.
- Microwave: Not suitable.

Plate and jug from Corso De' Fiori; glass from Freedom Furniture

Platter, jug and tile from Corso De' Fiori

GARLIC TOASTS WITH TWO TOPPINGS

200g salt cod
2 x 28cm long thin bread sticks
10 cloves garlic, halved
½ cup (125ml) olive oil
150g soft blue cheese, thinly sliced
2 tablespoons pine nuts, toasted
1 tablespoon fresh oregano leaves
5 artichoke hearts in oil,
    drained, quartered
1 tablespoon fresh flat-leaf
    parsley leaves

1. Place cod in medium bowl, cover with cold water. Cover bowl with plastic wrap, refrigerate 24 hours, changing water several times. Drain cod, add to medium pan of boiling water, simmer, uncovered, 1 minute. Drain, rinse under cold water; drain well.

2. Flake cod with fork; discard skin and any bones.

2. Cut bread into 1cm slices, toast both sides lightly. Rub garlic over 1 side of each toast then brush with half the oil. Top half the toasts with cheese, nuts and oregano; top remaining toasts with salt cod, artichokes and parsley. Drizzle remaining oil over toasts.

Makes about 40.

▨ Salt cod must be prepared
   24 hours ahead.
▨ Storage: Covered, in refrigerator.
▨ Freeze: Not suitable.
▨ Microwave: Not suitable.

QUAIL WITH TOMATOES AND MINT DRESSING

6 (1kg) quail
1 teaspoon ground cumin
3 cloves garlic, crushed
1/4 cup (60ml) olive oil
2 medium (380g) tomatoes,
**   seeded, chopped**

MINT DRESSING
1/2 cup (125ml) olive oil
1/3 cup (80ml) white wine vinegar
1 tablespoon shredded fresh
**   mint leaves**

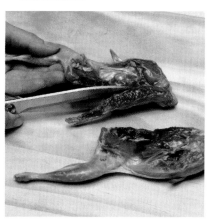

1. Halve quail between breasts; cut along either side of backbone, discard the backbone.

2. Cut each quail half into 2 pieces, combine with cumin, garlic and 1 tablespoon of the oil in large bowl.

3. Heat remaining oil in large pan, cook quail, in batches, until browned. Place quail, skin side up, in single layer on oven tray; bake uncovered in moderate oven about 15 minutes or until cooked.

4. Place quail in large bowl, pour over Mint Dressing; cover, refrigerate for 3 hours or overnight. Remove from refrigerator about 30 minutes before serving. Stir in tomatoes.
Mint Dressing: Combine all ingredients in jar; shake well.

Serves 6 to 8.

- Best made a day ahead.
- Storage: Covered, in refrigerator.
- Freeze: Not suitable.
- Microwave: Not suitable.

Patterned tiles from Bayteak Leisure Store; other tiles from Country Floors

35

SCRAMBLED EGG AND ASPARAGUS TARTLETS

1½ cups (225g) plain flour
125g butter, chopped
1 egg yolk
1 tablespoon iced water,
 approximately

FILLING
1 tablespoon olive oil
1 large (200g) onion, finely chopped
3 bacon rashers, finely chopped
1 bunch (250g) asparagus,
 finely chopped
1 small (150g) green pepper,
 finely chopped
1 medium (190g) tomato,
 seeded, chopped
5 eggs, lightly beaten
½ teaspoon cracked black pepper

1. Grease 2 x 12-hole shallow patty pans. Process flour and butter until crumbly, add egg yolk and enough water to make ingredients just cling together. Knead dough on floured surface until smooth, cover with plastic wrap, refrigerate 30 minutes.

2. Roll pastry between sheets of baking paper until 2mm thick, then cut into 24 x 6.5cm rounds. Ease rounds into patty pans; prick bases lightly with fork. Bake in moderately hot oven about 15 minutes or until lightly browned. Spoon hot filling into hot pastry cases.

3. **Filling:** Heat oil in medium pan; cook onion and bacon, stirring, until onion is soft. Add asparagus, green pepper and tomato; cook, stirring, 3 minutes. Add eggs and black pepper; cook over low heat, stirring occasionally, until almost set.

Makes 24.

▨ Best made just before serving.
▨ Freeze: Not suitable.
▨ Microwave: Filling suitable.

Wooden chest from Michele Shennen's Garden Centres

ARTICHOKES IN OREGANO VINAIGRETTE

**6 medium (1.2kg) fresh globe
   artichokes**
½ cup (125ml) lemon juice
⅓ cup (80ml) olive oil
1 tablespoon white wine vinegar
2 cloves garlic, crushed
**1 small (100g) red onion,
   thinly sliced**
**1 tablespoon chopped
   fresh oregano leaves**

1. Trim base of artichokes to sit flat. Remove tough outer leaves, cut tips from remaining leaves, then brush artichokes with half the juice.

2. Add artichokes to large pan of boiling water, add remaining juice. Boil, uncovered, 20 minutes or until tender; drain artichokes upside down, cool.

3. Pull away a few inside leaves, remove coarse centre with a spoon. Quarter artichokes lengthways, place in large bowl; pour over combined oil, vinegar and garlic. Cover, refrigerate 3 hours or overnight. Combine artichoke mixture with onion, sprinkle with oregano leaves.

Serves 6 to 8.

- Can be made a day ahead.
- Storage: Covered, in refrigerator.
- Freeze: Not suitable.
- Microwave: Artichokes suitable.

CRUMBED SARDINES WITH ROASTED TOMATO SAUCE

24 fresh sardine fillets
plain flour
4 eggs, lightly beaten
3½ cups (245g) stale breadcrumbs
½ cup chopped fresh parsley
¼ cup chopped fresh
    oregano leaves
vegetable oil, for deep-frying

ROASTED TOMATO SAUCE
6 medium (450g) egg tomatoes,
    roughly chopped
4 cloves garlic, peeled
2 tablespoons red wine vinegar
2 tablespoons brown sugar
1 large (200g) onion,
    roughly chopped
2 tablespoons olive oil

3. **Roasted Tomato Sauce:** Combine all ingredients in large baking dish. Bake, uncovered, in hot oven about 30 minutes or until onions are soft.

1. Toss sardines in flour, dip in eggs, then combined breadcrumbs and herbs.

4. Blend or process tomato mixture until smooth.

Serves 4 to 6.

■ Sardines can be prepared a day ahead. Roasted Tomato Sauce can be made a day ahead.
■ Storage: Covered, separately, in refrigerator.
■ Freeze: Not suitable.
■ Microwave: Not suitable.

2. Deep-fry sardines, in batches, in hot oil until browned and cooked through; drain on absorbent paper. Serve with Roasted Tomato Sauce.

Platter, bowl and glasses from Corso De' Fiori; napkin from Freedom Furniture

MARINATED OCTOPUS

1kg baby octopus
1 litre (4 cups) water
½ teaspoon black peppercorns
4 bay leaves
1 medium (150g) onion, chopped
½ small (75g) red pepper, chopped
½ small (75g) green pepper,
** chopped**
⅓ cup (80ml) olive oil
¼ cup (60ml) white wine vinegar
2 tablespoons brown sugar
½ teaspoon ground sweet paprika
2 cloves garlic, crushed

1. Remove and discard heads and beaks from octopus.

2. Quarter octopus to make equal-size pieces.

3. Combine water, peppercorns, bay leaves and onion in large pan; bring to boil, add octopus pieces and peppers, simmer, stirring, about 2 minutes or until octopus is tender. Strain octopus mixture over medium bowl; reserve ⅓ cup (80ml) cooking liquid, discard bay leaves. Cool.

Plates from Corso De' Fiori; jug from Bayteak Leisure Store

4. Combine reserved cooking liquid, oil, vinegar, sugar, paprika and garlic with octopus mixture; mix well. Cover, refrigerate overnight.

Serves 6 to 8.
■ Must be made a day ahead.
■ Storage: Covered, in refrigerator.
■ Freeze: Not suitable.
■ Microwave: Not suitable.

GARLIC CHICKEN PIECES

12 medium (1kg) chicken wings
1 tablespoon white wine vinegar
1 medium (150g) onion, thinly sliced
6 cloves garlic, crushed
2 small fresh red chillies,
    finely chopped
1 tablespoon ground sweet paprika
1 teaspoon ground hot paprika
1/4 cup (60ml) olive oil
1 tablespoon chopped fresh
    oregano leaves

2. Separate first and second joints of chicken wings.

4. Place chicken mixture, in a single layer in large shallow baking dish. Bake, uncovered, in moderate oven about 1 hour or until browned and cooked through. Stir in oregano.

Makes 24.

■ Can be prepared a day ahead.
■ Storage: Covered, in refrigerator.
■ Freeze: Marinated wings suitable.
■ Microwave: Not suitable.

1. Remove and discard wing tips from chicken wings.

3. Combine chicken with vinegar, onion, garlic, chillies, paprika and oil in medium bowl; cover, refrigerate for 3 hours or overnight.

PIMENTÓN

OCTOPUS WITH LEMON AND GARLIC

Order an octopus in advance from your fishmonger.

5kg octopus
500ml (2 cups) olive oil,
approximately
¼ cup (60ml) lemon juice
2 cloves garlic, crushed
2 tablespoons red wine vinegar
2 small fresh red chillies, chopped
1 teaspoon sugar
½ teaspoon cracked black pepper
½ cup (125ml) olive oil, extra
¼ cup chopped fresh
oregano leaves

3. Cover pan with inverted lid, weigh down with a brick or can. Simmer, about 1¼ hours or until octopus is tender. Drain octopus; discard oil.

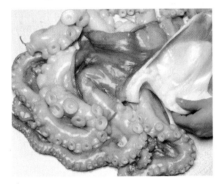

1. Remove head, beak and skin from the octopus.

4. Remove sinew and suckers from octopus by running hand along tentacles; cut octopus into 5mm slices.

2. Press octopus firmly into medium pan; it must be a tight fit. Pour in enough oil to barely cover octopus.

5. Place octopus in large bowl, pour over combined remaining ingredients. Cover, refrigerate 3 hours or overnight.

Serves 8 to 10.

- Can be made a day ahead.
- Storage: Covered, in refrigerator.
- Freeze: Not suitable.
- Microwave: Not suitable.

Wire basket and rug from Accoutrement

OPEN TOMATO AND PEPPER SANDWICHES

1 large round crusty Italian bread
**1/2 cup (75g) flaked
 manchego cheese**
150g jar anchovy fillets, drained
1/3 cup (80ml) olive oil

TOMATO TOPPING
**5 medium (950g) tomatoes, peeled,
 seeded, chopped**
2 tablespoons olive oil
1 clove garlic, crushed
**2 tablespoons chopped
 fresh parsley**

PEPPER TOPPING
2 large (600g) red peppers
2 tablespoons olive oil
1 teaspoon red wine vinegar

1. Cut bread into 1cm slices, toast half the slices both sides. Top toasted slices with Tomato Topping, sprinkle with cheese. Top untoasted slices with Pepper Topping, then with anchovies. Drizzle all sandwiches with oil.

2. Tomato Topping: Combine all ingredients in medium bowl.

3. Pepper Topping: Quarter peppers, remove seeds and membranes. Roast under grill or in very hot oven, skin side up, until skin blisters and blackens. Cover pepper pieces in plastic or paper for 5 minutes, then peel away skin, cut into 5mm slices. Combine peppers, oil and vinegar in medium bowl.

Makes about 40.

- Best made just before serving. Pepper Topping can be prepared a day ahead.
- Storage: Covered, in refrigerator.
- Freeze: Not suitable.
- Microwave: Not suitable.

44

POTATO WEDGES WITH CHILLI TOMATO SAUCE

7 medium (1.4kg) potatoes, halved
2 tablespoons olive oil
1 clove garlic, crushed
2 teaspoons fine sea salt

CHILLI TOMATO SAUCE
1 tablespoon olive oil
1 small (100g) red onion, chopped
1 clove garlic, crushed
1 small fresh red chilli, sliced
1 teaspoon ground sweet paprika
425g can tomatoes
2 tablespoons dry white wine
1 tablespoon tomato paste
1 tablespoon white wine vinegar
2 teaspoons sugar
1 tablespoon finely chopped
**   fresh parsley**

3. **Chilli Tomato Sauce:** Heat oil in medium pan, cook onion, garlic, chilli and paprika, stirring, until onion is soft. Add undrained crushed tomatoes, wine, paste, vinegar and sugar, simmer, uncovered, about 15 minutes or until thick. Blend or process tomato mixture until almost smooth, stir in parsley.

Serves about 10.
◼ Potato Wedges best made just before serving. Chilli Tomato Sauce can be made a day ahead.
◼ Storage: Covered, in refrigerator.
◼ Freeze: Not suitable.
◼ Microwave: Sauce suitable.

1. Cut each potato half into 3 wedges; toss wedges with remaining ingredients in large bowl.

2. Place wedges in a single layer in baking dishes; bake, uncovered, in moderately hot oven about 1¼ hours or until browned and crisp. Serve with Chilli Tomato Sauce.

Tile mosaic from Tilescope of Mosman

SOUPS

Traditionally, soup has always held an important position on the Spanish menu, and these recipes prove why. From subtle and light, even cold, versions to more complex and robust stockpots, soups can either begin a multi-course meal or star as a one-dish dinner, accompanied only by a warm loaf of bread.

CHICKPEA, GARLIC AND MINT SOUP

2 teaspoons olive oil
2 medium (300g) onions, chopped
2 litres (8 cups) chicken stock
2 tablespoons white wine vinegar
2 x 425g cans chickpeas, drained
1 teaspoon ground cumin
5 cloves garlic, crushed
2 large (500g) tomatoes,
    seeded, chopped
2 tablespoons shredded fresh mint

CRISPY BREAD
8 slices white bread
¼ cup (60ml) olive oil

1. Heat oil in large pan, add onions, cook, stirring, until soft and lightly browned. Add stock and vinegar; bring to boil. Add the chickpeas and cumin, simmer, uncovered, 15 minutes.

2. Add garlic, tomatoes and fresh mint, simmer, uncovered about 5 minutes or until tomatoes are soft. Serve with Crispy Bread.

3. Crispy Bread: Trim and discard crusts from bread; brush with oil. Cook bread, in batches, in heated griddle pan until browned. Place bread on oven tray, bake in moderate oven about 5 minutes or until crisp; cut in half diagonally.

Serves 6.

■ Soup can be made a day ahead. Crispy Bread best made just before serving.
■ Storage: Covered, in refrigerator.
■ Freeze: Not suitable.
■ Microwave: Not suitable.

ROASTED EGGPLANT AND PEPPER SOUP

3 large (1.5kg) eggplants
1 large (350g) red pepper
1 tablespoon olive oil
1 large (200g) onion, chopped
4 cloves garlic, chopped
3 medium (570g) tomatoes,
    chopped
1 teaspoon ground cumin
1 teaspoon ground sweet paprika
1.5 litres (6 cups) chicken stock
1/4 cup (60ml) lemon juice

RED PEPPER CREAM
1 large (350g) red pepper
1 large (200g) onion, quartered
1½ tablespoons water
½ cup (125ml) thickened cream

3. Heat oil in large pan, add onion and garlic, cook, stirring, until onion is soft. Add eggplant, pepper, tomatoes, cumin and paprika; stir for 2 minutes. Add stock and juice, simmer, uncovered, about 20 minutes or until vegetables are just soft.

1. Pierce eggplants several times with skewer, place on oven tray then roast, uncovered, in hot oven, 45 minutes or until soft. Cool 15 minutes, then peel eggplants, chop flesh.

4. Blend or process until smooth, press through fine strainer; discard pulp. Return soup to same pan, stir until hot; top with Red Pepper Cream.

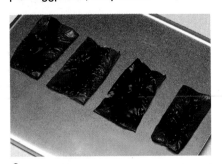

2. Quarter pepper, remove seeds and membranes. Roast under grill or in very hot oven, skin side up, until skin blisters and blackens. Cover pepper pieces in plastic or paper for 5 minutes, peel away skin, chop pepper.

5. Red Pepper Cream: Prepare red pepper as in Step 2. Grill or roast onion until soft. Blend or process pepper, onion and water until smooth. Press pepper mixture through fine strainer, discard pulp. Beat cream in small bowl with electric mixer until soft peaks form, fold in pepper mixture.

Serves 6.

- Soup and Red Pepper Cream can be made a day ahead.
- Storage: Covered, separately, in refrigerator.
- Freeze: Not suitable.
- Microwave: Not suitable.

Tiles from Fred Pazotti

SPICY SPINACH, POTATO AND BROAD BEAN SOUP

1 tablespoon olive oil
1 large (300g) red onion, chopped
2 cloves garlic, crushed
3 teaspoons ground sweet paprika
2 teaspoons ground cumin
1 teaspoon ground coriander
½ teaspoon ground cinnamon
425g can tomatoes
4 medium (800g) potatoes, chopped
1.5 litres (6 cups) vegetable stock
1 bunch (500g) English spinach, chopped
500g packet frozen broad beans, thawed, peeled

1. Heat oil in large pan, add the onion, garlic and spices; cook, stirring, until onion is soft.

2. Add undrained crushed tomatoes, potatoes and stock, simmer, covered, stirring occasionally, about 20 minutes or until potatoes are just tender. Add spinach and broad beans then simmer, uncovered, until spinach is wilted.

Serves 6.

▨ Can be made a day ahead.
▨ Storage: Covered, in refrigerator.
▨ Freeze: Suitable.
▨ Microwave: Suitable.

Saucepan from Bondi Storehouse

SPINACH, PRAWN AND SMOKED SALMON SOUP

750g uncooked medium prawns
1.5 litres (6 cups) water
1 cup (250ml) dry white wine
2 tablespoons olive oil
2 medium (300g) onions, chopped
6 cloves garlic, crushed
1 teaspoon plain flour
¼ cup (60ml) fish stock
1 bunch (500g) English spinach,
    roughly chopped
¼ cup chopped fresh parsley
½ cup (125ml) cream
200g smoked salmon,
    roughly chopped

1. Shell and devein prawns; reserve shells. Roughly chop prawns and reserve. Combine prawn shells, water and wine in medium pan, simmer, uncovered, 20 minutes, strain prawn stock into bowl; discard shells.

2. Heat oil in large pan, add onions and garlic, cook, stirring, until onions are soft. Add flour, cook, stirring, until mixture is dry and grainy. Gradually add prawn stock, stirring until mixture boils and thickens slightly. Add fish stock and spinach, stir over heat, until spinach is wilted.

3. Blend or process spinach mixture, in batches, until smooth; combine with prawns and remaining ingredients in large pan, stir until heated through.

Serves 6.
■ Best made just before serving. Prawn stock can be made a day ahead.
■ Storage: Covered, in refrigerator.
■ Freeze: Not suitable.
■ Microwave: Not suitable.

GAZPACHO

5 slices white bread
1 clove garlic, crushed
1/3 cup (80ml) olive oil
1/4 cup (60ml) red wine vinegar
4 large (1kg) ripe tomatoes,
    peeled, chopped
2 medium (340g) Lebanese
    cucumbers, peeled, chopped
1 medium (200g) red pepper,
    chopped
1 medium (170g) red onion,
    chopped
1/3 cup (80ml) orange juice
1 small (100g) red onion,
    finely chopped, extra
1 small (150g) red pepper,
    finely chopped, extra
1 small (130g) Lebanese cucumber,
    seeded, finely chopped, extra
1 tablespoon chopped fresh parsley
12 ice cubes

CROUTONS
2 slices white bread
2 tablespoons olive oil

2. Blend or process bread mixture with tomatoes, cucumbers, pepper, onion and juice until smooth. Press mixture through fine strainer; discard pulp. Cover, refrigerate 3 hours or overnight. Just before serving, top soup with extra onion, extra pepper, extra cucumber, parsley, ice cubes and Croutons.

1. Trim and discard crusts from bread, tear into pieces. Combine bread, garlic, oil and vinegar in medium bowl, stand 30 minutes.

3. Croutons: Trim and discard crusts from bread, cut into small cubes. Heat oil in medium pan, add bread cubes, stir until just browned and crisp; drain on absorbent paper.

Serves 6.

- Gazpacho and Croutons can be made a day ahead.
- Storage: Gazpacho, covered, in refrigerator. Croutons, in airtight container.
- Freeze: Not suitable.
- Microwave: Not suitable.

Pepper grinder and wire basket from Accoutrement

WHITE GAZPACHO
WITH GRAPES

5 slices white bread
1/2 cup (125ml) white wine vinegar
1/2 cup (125ml) olive oil
1 small (80g) onion, finely chopped
3 cloves garlic, crushed
1 cup (160g) blanched almonds
1/2 cup (125ml) cream
3 1/2 cups (875ml) water
400g seedless white grapes
1 medium (170g) Lebanese
    cucumber, seeded, chopped

1. Trim crusts from bread; discard crusts, place bread in medium bowl, pour over vinegar. Stand for 10 minutes then squeeze excess moisture from bread.

2. Heat oil in small pan, add onion and garlic; cook, stirring, until onion is soft.

3. Combine bread, onion mixture, nuts, cream, water and half the grapes in bowl. Blend or process mixture, in batches, until smooth. Transfer mixture to medium bowl, cover, refrigerate for 3 hours or overnight. Just before serving, stir in cucumber and remaining grapes.

Serves 6.

▧ Can be made a day ahead.
▧ Storage: Covered, in refrigerator.
▧ Freeze: Not suitable.
▧ Microwave: Onion mixture suitable.

WINTER SOUP WITH OXTAIL AND CHICKPEAS

2 tablespoons olive oil
1kg chopped oxtail
4 medium (480g) carrots, chopped
1 small (200g) leek, finely sliced
4 cloves garlic, sliced
2 sticks celery, chopped
¼ cup (60ml) tomato paste
3 bay leaves
2 litres (8 cups) beef stock
1 (170g) chorizo sausage, chopped
425g can chickpeas, rinsed, drained
½ cup (125g) stelline pasta (star-shaped)

1. Heat oil in large pan, cook oxtail, in batches, stirring until browned all over; remove from pan.

2. Add carrots, leek, garlic and celery to same pan, cook, stirring, until leek is soft. Add oxtail, paste, bay leaves and stock; simmer, uncovered, for about 3 hours or until meat is tender. Strain soup into a large bowl, remove oxtail from the vegetable mixture then return vegetable mixture to bowl. Remove meat from oxtail; discard the bones, return meat to soup; cool. Cover bowl; refrigerate overnight.

3. Remove fat from surface of soup, return soup to pan. Place sausage in small heated pan; cook, stirring, until just crisp then drain on absorbent paper. Stir sausage, chickpeas and pasta into soup mixture; simmer, covered, about 8 minutes or until pasta is just tender.

Serves 6 to 8.

- Must be made a day ahead.
- Storage: Covered, in refrigerator.
- Freeze: Suitable.
- Microwave: Not suitable.

Casserole from House

SPICY LEMON SEAFOOD SOUP

500g uncooked medium prawns
250g white fish fillets
200g calamari hoods
2 teaspoons olive oil
1 large (300g) red onion,
    halved, sliced
2 cloves garlic, crushed
1½ tablespoons grated lemon rind
3 bay leaves
1 teaspoon ground sweet paprika
2 small fresh red chillies, sliced
½ cup (125ml)) dry white wine
¼ cup (60ml) lemon juice
2 litres (8 cups) fish stock
2 tablespoons roughly chopped
    fresh flat-leaf parsley
2 green onions, chopped

2. Heat oil in large pan, add red onion and garlic, cook, stirring, until onion is soft. Add rind, bay leaves, paprika, chillies, wine, juice and stock; simmer, uncovered, 20 minutes.

1. Peel and devein prawns, leaving tails intact. Cut fish and calamari into 2cm pieces.

3. Add seafood, parsley and green onions, simmer, uncovered, 2 minutes or until seafood is just cooked; discard bay leaves.

Serves 6 to 8.

▓ Must be made just before serving.
▓ Freeze: Not suitable.
▓ Microwave: Not suitable.

Soup tureen from Accoutrement; breadboard from Bondi Storehouse

LENTIL SOUP

2 tablespoons olive oil
4 cloves garlic, finely chopped
150g piece ham, chopped
1 large (200g) onion, chopped
2 sticks celery, sliced
1 medium (120g) carrot, chopped
1 medium (200g) potato, chopped
2½ cups (500g) brown lentils
4 litres (16 cups) water
2 bay leaves
4 large (1kg) tomatoes, chopped
¼ cup (60ml) red wine vinegar
1½ teaspoons ground
    sweet paprika

1. Heat oil in large pan, add garlic, ham, onion, celery, carrot and potato; cook, stirring, until vegetables are soft. Remove from pan; reserve.

2. Add lentils, water and bay leaves to same pan, simmer, uncovered, about 30 minutes or until the lentils are almost tender. Stir in the reserved vegetable mixture and tomatoes then simmer, uncovered, about 30 minutes or until soup thickens slightly and lentils are just soft. Add vinegar and paprika, stir until heated through.

Serves 8 to 10.

▧ Can be made a day ahead.
▧ Storage: Covered, in refrigerator.
▧ Freeze: Suitable.
▧ Microwave: Suitable.

Bowls from Accoutrement

58

SMOKED HAM, TOMATO AND BUTTER BEAN SOUP

1 tablespoon olive oil
1 large (300g) red onion, chopped
2 cloves garlic, crushed
700g smoked ham bone
6 medium (1.1kg) tomatoes, peeled,
    seeded, chopped
2 medium (240g) carrots, chopped
1.5 litres (6 cups) chicken stock
3 x 300g cans butter beans,
    rinsed, drained
2 tablespoons chopped fresh mint

1. Heat oil in large pan, add onion and garlic, cook, stirring, until onion is soft.

2. Trim fat from ham bone. Add ham bone, tomatoes, carrots and stock to pan; simmer, covered, about 2 hours, stirring occasionally, or until ham comes away from bone.

3. Remove meat from ham bone, chop finely; discard bone. Return meat to pan with beans and mint, stir until heated through.

Serves 6.

■ Can be made a day ahead.
■ Storage: Covered, in refrigerator.
■ Freeze: Suitable.
■ Microwave: Not suitable.

MAINS

Ingredients from the New World and Mid-Eastern cooking influenced the already classic, elegant main courses of Spain, resulting in a wealth of recipes now popular worldwide. From paella to lentils with chorizo to a heady seafood casserole, these main dishes will bring a loud "Ole!" from your family and friends.

OLIVE CITRUS LAMB SHANKS

8 (1.5kg) lamb shanks
1½ tablespoons plain flour
½ teaspoon cracked black pepper
2 tablespoons olive oil
1 large (300g) red onion
4 cloves garlic, crushed
2 teaspoons ground sweet paprika
6 medium (1kg) tomatoes, peeled, seeded, quartered
3 large (540g) carrots, chopped
2 tablespoons tomato paste
2 teaspoons sugar
1 cup (250ml) dry red wine
½ cup (125ml) water
1 tablespoon beef stock powder
2 sprigs fresh rosemary
3 strips lemon rind
1 cinnamon stick
¾ cup (90g) seeded black olives
2 tablespoons lemon juice
2 tablespoons chopped fresh mint

1. Toss lamb in combined flour and pepper. Heat oil in large pan, cook lamb, in batches, until browned all over; drain on absorbent paper.

2. Cut onion in half lengthways, slice into thick wedges. Add onion, garlic and paprika to same pan, cook, stirring, until onions are just soft.

3. Return lamb to pan; add tomatoes, carrots, paste, sugar, wine, water, stock powder, rosemary, rind and cinnamon. Simmer, covered, 1½ hours, stirring occasionally. Stir in olives, simmer, uncovered, about 30 minutes, or until lamb shanks are tender. Just before serving, stir in juice and mint.

Serves 4.

■ Can be made a day ahead.
■ Storage: Covered, in refrigerator.
■ Freeze: Suitable.
■ Microwave: Not suitable.

DUCK SEVILLE-STYLE

6 (900g) duck breast fillets
12 (360g) baby onions
4 cloves garlic, crushed
6 sprigs fresh thyme
½ cup (125ml) dry sherry
1½ cups (375ml) chicken stock
2 bay leaves
2 medium (360g) oranges, sliced
2 cups (300g) large green
    olives, seeded
1 tablespoon cornflour
1 tablespoon water

1. Trim fat from duck. Place duck, skin side down, in large pan; cook, until skin is brown and crisp, and the fat melted. Drain duck on absorbent paper; place in 9-cup (2.25-litre) ovenproof dish. Remove all but 2 teaspoons fat from pan.

2. Add onions to the same pan; cook, stirring, until browned. Add garlic; cook, stirring, until fragrant. Add thyme, sherry, stock, bay leaves and orange slices; bring to boil.

3. Pour orange mixture over duck; bake, covered, in moderate oven about 1½ hours or until tender. Remove duck, onions and oranges from dish, cover to keep warm.

4. Strain juices from dish into medium pan, add olives and blended cornflour and water. Stir over heat until sauce boils and thickens, simmer, uncovered, about 5 minutes or until the sauce is slightly reduced. Serve sauce over duck, onions and oranges.

Serves 6.

■ Duck and sauce can be made
    a day ahead.
■ Storage: Covered, separately,
    in refrigerator.
■ Freeze: Not suitable.
■ Microwave: Not suitable.

Tiles from Country Floors; platter from Orson & Blake Collectables

SEAFOOD CASSEROLE

1kg small mussels
1kg uncooked prawns
500g calamari hoods
500g uncooked lobster tail
1 tablespoon olive oil
1 medium (350g) leek, sliced
4 cloves garlic, crushed
425g can tomatoes
3/4 cup (180ml) dry white wine
1/4 cup (60ml) sweet sherry
2 cups (500ml) fish stock
pinch saffron threads
2 medium (240g) carrots, chopped
1/3 cup chopped fresh parsley
1 tablespoon chopped fresh thyme
350g scallops

1. Scrub mussels, remove beards. Shell and devein prawns, leaving tails intact. Cut calamari open, score shallow diagonal pattern on inside surface, cut into 6cm pieces. Shell lobster tail, cut lobster meat into 5cm pieces.

2. Heat oil in large pan, add leek and garlic; cook, stirring, until leek is soft.

3. Add undrained crushed tomatoes, wine, sherry, stock, saffron, carrots and herbs; simmer, covered, 30 minutes.

4. Add mussels; simmer, covered, 2 minutes. Add prawns, calamari and lobster pieces; simmer, covered, about 2 minutes. Add the scallops; simmer, uncovered, about 2 minutes or until seafood is just cooked. Discard any unopened mussels.

Serves 6 to 8.

■ Best made just before serving.
■ Freeze: Not suitable.
■ Microwave: Not suitable.

Tiles from Country Floors

CHICKEN WITH ALMOND SAUCE

¼ cup (60ml) olive oil
½ cup (125ml) orange juice
3 cloves garlic, crushed
6 (1kg) single chicken breast fillets
1 tablespoon olive oil, extra
1 medium (620g) fennel bulb, sliced
1 bunch (400g) spring
   onions, halved

ALMOND SAUCE
1 tablespoon olive oil
¼ cup (15g) stale breadcrumbs
¾ cup (90g) ground almonds
pinch ground cloves
1 cup (250ml) chicken stock
2 tablespoons dry white wine
¼ cup (60ml) thickened cream

1. Combine oil, juice, garlic and chicken in a medium bowl; cover, refrigerate 3 hours or overnight.

2. Heat extra oil in large pan, add fennel and onions; cook, stirring, until onions are soft and lightly browned. Remove from heat, cover to keep warm. Add drained chicken to heated greased griddle pan (or grill or barbecue); cook, in batches, until browned both sides and just cooked. Serve chicken with fennel mixture and Almond Sauce.

Woven bowl and urn from Orson & Blake Collectables

3. Almond Sauce: Heat oil in pan, add breadcrumbs, cook, stirring, until lightly browned. Add almonds and cloves; cook, stirring, until lightly browned. Gradually add combined stock and wine, stir over heat until mixture is smooth; bring to boil. Remove from heat, stir in cream.

Serves 6.
▨ Best made just before serving.
▨ Freeze: Not suitable.
▨ Microwave: Not suitable.

PAELLA

10 (850g) chicken wings
500g clams
2 teaspoons coarse cooking salt
500g medium uncooked prawns
500g small mussels
1 teaspoon saffron threads
1½ cups (375ml) dry white wine
2 tablespoons olive oil
2 (340g) chorizo sausages, sliced
1 large (300g) red onion, chopped
3 cups (600g) calrose rice
1 large (350g) red pepper, chopped
4 medium (760g) tomatoes, peeled,
**   seeded, chopped**
4½ cups (1.125litres) chicken stock
400g green beans, chopped
500g scallops
1 cup (125g) frozen peas

1. Remove and discard wing tips from chicken, separate first and second joints. Rinse clams under cold water, place in large bowl, sprinkle with salt, cover with cold water; soak 1½ hours. Discard water, rinse and drain clams. Shell and devein prawns, leaving tails intact. Scrub mussels, remove beards.

2. Combine saffron and wine in glass jug; stand 30 minutes.

3. Heat oil in large pan, add chicken, cook until browned and tender; remove from pan. Add sausages to same pan, cook, stirring, until browned; drain on absorbent paper. Add onion to same pan, cook, stirring, until soft. Add the saffron mixture, rice and pepper, cook, stirring, until wine is absorbed. Add tomatoes and about 1 cup (250ml) stock, cook, stirring, until stock is absorbed. Add remaining stock, cook, stirring, until mixture boils and rice is almost tender.

4. Place clams, prawns, mussels, sausages and beans over rice mixture, simmer, covered, 5 minutes. Add chicken, scallops and peas, cook, covered, about 10 minutes or until scallops are just cooked through. Stand, covered, for another 5 minutes before serving.

Serves 8.

◼ Best made just before serving.
◼ Freeze: Not suitable.
◼ Microwave: Not suitable.

ASTURIAN-STYLE LAMB AND VEGETABLES

2kg leg of lamb, butterflied
1/4 cup chopped fresh mint
2 tablespoons chopped
    fresh parsley
1/2 cup (125ml) olive oil
4 cloves garlic, crushed
1/4 cup (60ml) red wine vinegar
1 teaspoon ground sweet paprika
1 tablespoon sugar
1/2 teaspoon cracked black pepper
500g baby new potatoes, halved
1 medium (170g) red onion, sliced
1 medium (350g) leek, sliced
60g butter, melted

1. Pound lamb with meat mallet until an even thickness all over.

2. Combine lamb with herbs, oil, garlic, vinegar, paprika, sugar and pepper in large bowl; cover, refrigerate for about 3 hours or overnight.

3. Place potatoes, onion and leek in large baking dish; drizzle with butter. Bake in moderately hot oven about 20 minutes or until potatoes are slightly tender. Remove lamb from marinade; place, skin side up, over vegetables in dish. Bake in moderately hot oven about 40 minutes or until lamb is tender. Remove lamb, onion and leek from baking dish, cover to keep warm. Drain away excess pan juices then bake the potatoes in very hot oven about 10 minutes or until crisp. Slice lamb and serve with vegetables.

Serves 6 to 8.

■ Best made just before serving.
■ Freeze: Not suitable.
■ Microwave: Not suitable.

Plate from Bondi Storehouse

MEDITERRANEAN SNAPPER WITH ROASTED TOMATOES

8 medium (600g) egg
   tomatoes, halved
4 large (1.2kg) potatoes,
   thickly sliced
1 large (300g) red onion
1 tablespoon olive oil
4 cloves garlic, crushed
1/3 cup chopped fresh chives
3 teaspoons chopped fresh thyme
1.5kg whole snapper
1/3 cup (50g) seeded black olives
1/2 cup (125ml) dry white wine
2 tablespoons olive oil, extra
1/4 cup (60ml) lemon juice
1/2 teaspoon sugar
1/4 cup (15g) stale breadcrumbs,
   toasted

1. Place tomatoes, cut side up, on wire rack over baking dish. Bake, uncovered, in hot oven for about 30 minutes. Place potatoes in large pan of boiling water; boil, uncovered, about 5 minutes or until potatoes are almost tender; drain.

2. Cut onion in half lengthways, slice into thick wedges. Heat oil in medium pan, add onion, garlic and herbs; cook, stirring, until onion is soft.

Tiles from Country Floors

3. Cut 3 shallow slashes across fish on both sides. Place potatoes in large, greased 4-litre (16-cup) ovenproof dish,

top with onion mixture. Place fish on onion mixture, place tomatoes and olives around fish. Pour combined wine, extra oil, juice and sugar over fish; sprinkle with breadcrumbs. Bake, uncovered, in moderately hot oven about 40 minutes or until fish is just cooked.

Serves 4.

▨ Best made just before serving.
▨ Freeze: Not suitable.
▨ Microwave: Not suitable.

PINE NUT AND SPINACH ROLLED LAMB LOIN

Ask your butcher to bone out a double loin of lamb, fillets left in, boned weight about 1.5kg. This cut is called a baron of lamb by many butchers.

2 tablespoons olive oil
2 small (200g) red onions, thinly sliced
2 cloves garlic, crushed
2 teaspoons ground cumin
2 teaspoons ground sweet paprika
½ teaspoon ground cinnamon
¼ teaspoon cayenne pepper
2 tablespoons chopped fresh oregano
¼ cup (40g) chopped raisins
2 tablespoons pine nuts, toasted
1 bunch (500g) English spinach
1.5kg double loin of lamb, boned
1½ tablespoons plain flour
½ cup (125ml) dry white wine
1 cup (250ml) water
3 teaspoons chicken stock powder
½ teaspoon sugar

1. Heat half the oil in medium pan, add onions, garlic, spices and oregano; cook, stirring, about 5 minutes or until onions are soft. Stir in raisins and pine nuts; cook 1 minute then cool.

2. Boil, steam or microwave spinach until just wilted; drain, squeeze out excess liquid, chop. Open lamb out on flat surface, fat side down; spread onion mixture over lamb, top with spinach. Roll lamb up tightly from short end; tie with string at 2cm intervals.

3. Heat remaining oil in large baking dish; add lamb, cook until browned all over. Bake, uncovered, in moderately hot oven, about 40 minutes or until cooked as desired. Remove lamb from dish, cover to keep warm.

4. Add flour to juices in dish, stir over heat, until the mixture bubbles. Add combined wine, water, stock powder and sugar, stir over heat, until gravy boils and thickens; strain. Serve lamb with gravy.

Serves 4 to 6.

■ Best made just before serving.
■ Freeze: Not suitable.
■ Microwave: Spinach suitable.

Tiles from Country Floors

LEMON AND OLIVE CRISPY CHICKEN

4 (1kg) single chicken breasts
  on bone
1 teaspoon grated lemon rind
2 tablespoons lemon juice
2 cloves garlic, crushed
1/3 cup (50g) plain flour
1 teaspoon ground cumin
1 teaspoon ground coriander
3 teaspoons chopped fresh thyme
1 tablespoon olive oil

LEMON OLIVE MIXTURE
2 medium (280g) lemons
1/3 cup (80ml) olive oil
2 cloves garlic, crushed
3/4 cup (90g) seeded black olives
4 large (360g) egg tomatoes, sliced
1 tablespoon white wine vinegar

3. **Lemon Olive Mixture:** Cut lemons in half lengthways, slice thinly. Heat oil in medium pan, add garlic; cook, stirring, until fragrant. Add the lemons, olives, tomatoes and vinegar, stir gently until just warmed through.

Serves 4.

▨ Chicken best made just before serving. Lemon Olive Mixture can be made a day ahead.
▨ Storage: Covered, in refrigerator.
▨ Freeze: Not suitable.
▨ Microwave: Not suitable.

1. Combine chicken, rind, juice and garlic in medium bowl; cover, refrigerate 3 hours or overnight.

2. Drain chicken; pat dry with absorbent paper. Coat chicken in combined flour, spices and thyme. Heat oil in large pan, add chicken, cook until browned and crisp both sides. Place chicken on oven tray, bake in moderately hot oven about 15 minutes or until just tender. Serve with Lemon Olive Mixture.

Plate from Bondi Storehouse

SPICY PORK WITH CARAMELISED ONIONS

1 tablespoon olive oil
2 large (400g) onions,
    finely chopped
1 small (150g) red pepper,
    finely chopped
4 slices (60g) prosciutto, chopped
1kg pork fillets
2 tablespoons olive oil, extra

1 teaspoon dried crushed chillies
1 tablespoon ground sweet paprika
2 teaspoons ground cumin

CARAMELISED ONIONS
2 tablespoons olive oil
3 large (600g) onions, sliced
¼ cup (60ml) red wine vinegar
120g guava paste, chopped
1 tablespoon chopped fresh
    coriander leaves
1 tablespoon brown sugar

1. Heat oil in large pan, add onions, pepper and prosciutto; cook, stirring, until onions are soft. Remove from pan.

2. Slice pork fillets lengthways down the centre, almost all the way through. Open each fillet flat, pound gently with a meat mallet until an even thickness. Spoon the onion mixture along centre of pork, roll up from long side; secure with toothpicks.

Heat extra oil in pan, add chillies and spices; cook, stirring, until fragrant. Add pork, cook, uncovered, turning occasionally, about 20 minutes or until just tender. While pork is cooking, make Caramelised Onions. Serve with Spicy Pork immediately.

3. Caramelised Onions: Heat oil in large pan; cook onions, stirring, about 15 minutes or until onions are very soft and a rich caramel colour. Add remaining ingredients, cook, stirring until guava paste and sugar are dissolved.

Serves 4 to 6.

■ Best made just before serving.
■ Freeze: Not suitable.
■ Microwave: Not suitable.

Bottle holder, placemat and pewter bowl from Home & Garden on the Mall; tiles from Domus Ceramics

SPATCHCOCK WITH CHOCOLATE SAUCE

6 x 500g spatchcocks
plain flour
1/4 cup (60ml) olive oil
1 medium (150g) onion, chopped
2 cloves garlic, crushed
1 cinnamon stick
1/4 teaspoon ground cloves
1/2 teaspoon ground nutmeg
2 x 425g cans tomatoes
1 large (350g) red pepper, sliced
1 cup (250ml) dry white wine
60g bittersweet chocolate,
    finely chopped

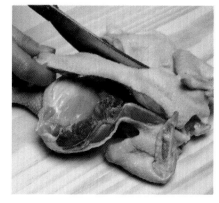

1. Cut along both sides of spatchcock backbones, discard backbones. Cut in half between breasts then cut each half into 2 pieces. Pat spatchcock pieces dry with absorbent paper; toss in flour.

2. Heat oil in large shallow pan; cook spatchcock, in batches, until browned. Drain on absorbent paper. Add onion and garlic to same pan, cook, stirring, until onion is soft. Add spices, cook, stirring, until fragrant.

Serving dish from Corso De' Fiori; tiles from Country Floors

3. Return spatchcock to pan with undrained crushed tomatoes, pepper and wine; simmer, covered, 20 minutes. Remove the cover, simmer another 20 minutes or until spatchcock is very tender and sauce thickened slightly. Add the chocolate, cook, stirring, until melted. Discard cinnamon stick.

Serves 6.

▨ Can be made a day ahead.
▨ Storage: Covered, in refrigerator.
▨ Freeze: Not suitable.
▨ Microwave: Not suitable.

TOMATO, CHORIZO AND SPINACH PIZZA

2 teaspoons (7g) dried yeast
1 teaspoon sugar
3/4 cup (180ml) warm water
2 cups (300g) plain flour
1 teaspoon salt
2 tablespoons olive oil
1 tablespoon chopped
    fresh oregano
1 (170g) chorizo sausage,
    thinly sliced
1 bunch (500g) English spinach
1 cup (200g) flaked
    manchego cheese
2 tablespoons pine nuts, toasted

TOMATO SAUCE
1 large (300g) red onion
2 teaspoons olive oil
2 cloves garlic, crushed
4 medium (760g) tomatoes, peeled,
    seeded, chopped
1 large (350g) red pepper, chopped
1/3 cup (80ml) tomato paste
1 1/2 tablespoons water
1 teaspoon sugar
2 tablespoons chopped
    fresh oregano

3. Turn dough onto floured surface, knead until smooth. Roll dough into 30cm x 35cm rectangle, place on greased oven tray. Add chorizo to medium heated pan, cook, stirring, until browned and crisp; drain on absorbent paper. Boil, steam or microwave spinach until just wilted; drain, squeeze out excess liquid, chop.

4. Spoon Tomato Sauce over dough, leaving a 1.5cm border. Sprinkle dough with half the cheese, top with chorizo, spinach, pine nuts and the remaining cheese. Bake in very hot oven about 20 minutes or until browned.

1. Combine yeast, sugar and water in small bowl. Cover; stand in warm place about 10 minutes or until frothy.

2. Sift flour and salt into large bowl, add yeast mixture, oil and oregano; mix to a firm dough. Knead dough on floured surface about 10 minutes or until smooth and elastic. Place dough in oiled bowl; cover, stand in warm place about 1 hour or until dough is doubled in size.

5. Tomato Sauce: Cut onion in half lengthways, slice into thick wedges. Heat oil in medium pan, add onion and garlic; cook, stirring, until the onion is soft. Stir in the remaining ingredients; simmer, uncovered, about 15 minutes or until thickened.

Serves 6.

■ Pizza best made just before serving. Tomato Sauce can be made a day ahead.
■ Storage: Covered, in refrigerator.
■ Freeze: Suitable.
■ Microwave: Spinach suitable.

CHICKEN IN ALMOND POMEGRANATE SAUCE

2 medium (640g) pomegranates
1½ cups (375ml) water
⅓ cup (65g) firmly packed
   brown sugar
2 tablespoons olive oil
4 (680g) single chicken breast fillets
1 large (200g) onion, thickly sliced
2 cloves garlic, crushed
1 tablespoon plain flour
1 teaspoon ground sweet paprika
1 teaspoon ground cumin
1 teaspoon ground coriander
½ teaspoon ground cinnamon
½ cup (125ml) chicken stock
⅓ cup (55g) blanched
   almonds, toasted
⅓ cup chopped fresh
   coriander leaves

3. Heat remaining oil in same pan; cook onion and garlic, stirring, until onion is soft. Add flour and spices; cook, stirring, about 1 minute or until mixture is just browned and dry. Gradually stir in stock and reserved pomegranate liquid; cook, stirring, until mixture boils and thickens slightly.

1. Cut pomegranates in half, scoop out seeds. Reserve about ⅓ cup seeds; combine remaining seeds, water and sugar in small pan, stir over heat, without boiling, until sugar is dissolved. Simmer, uncovered, 5 minutes; strain into a jug, reserve.

4. Return chicken to pan; simmer, covered, about 5 minutes or until cooked through. Stir in reserved pomegranate seeds, nuts and coriander.

Serves 4.

■ Best made just before serving.
■ Freeze: Not suitable.
■ Microwave: Not suitable.

2. Heat half the oil in large pan, cook chicken until browned both sides and almost cooked. Remove from pan.

Plates, placemat and fabric from *At Home Between the Sheets*

VEAL WITH CREAMY BLUE-CHEESE SAUCE

8 (750g) boneless veal steaks
½ cup chopped fresh parsley
¼ cup chopped fresh oregano
1 tablespoon chopped fresh
    rosemary leaves
2 tablespoons olive oil
1 large (200g) onion, sliced
4 cloves garlic, crushed
¼ cup (60ml) dry white wine
130g soft blue cheese
300ml cream

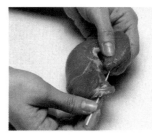

1. Skewer ends of each veal steak together with toothpick to make a round.

2. Roll outside edge of veal rounds in combined herbs. Heat oil in large pan, cook veal, in batches, until browned both sides and just cooked. Remove from pan, discard toothpicks, cover veal to keep warm.

3. Add onion and garlic to same pan; cook, stirring, until onion is soft. Add remaining ingredients; cook, stirring, without boiling, until cheese is melted. Top veal with blue-cheese sauce.

Serves 4 to 6.

■ Best made just before serving.
■ Freeze: Not suitable.
■ Microwave: Not suitable.

Platter from Country Floors; napkin from Corso De' Fiori

LENTIL AND CHORIZO SOFRITO

1 tablespoon olive oil
4 (680g) chorizo sausages, sliced
1 medium (150g) onion, chopped
6 bacon rashers, chopped
2 cloves garlic, crushed
2½ cups (500g) brown lentils
2 medium (240g) carrots, chopped
1kg baby new potatoes, halved
2 bay leaves
6 cups (1.5 litres) water
4 medium (480g) zucchini, sliced
¼ cup chopped fresh parsley

SOFRITO
4 medium (300g) egg tomatoes,
    peeled
1 tablespoon olive oil
1 large (300g) red onion, sliced

1. Heat oil in large pan, cook sausages, in batches, until browned; drain on absorbent paper. Add onion, bacon and garlic to same pan; cook, stirring, until onion is soft.

2. Return sausages to pan with lentils, carrots, potatoes, bay leaves and water; simmer, covered, about 40 minutes, stirring occasionally, until lentils are tender and mixture is thick. Add zucchini, simmer, covered, for about 10 minutes or until zucchini is tender. Serve lentil mixture topped with Sofrito and parsley.

3. Sofrito: Cut tomatoes into 8 wedges. Heat oil in pan, add onion, cook, stirring, about 20 minutes or until onion is browned and soft. Add tomatoes, cook, stirring gently, until tomatoes just begin to lose shape.

Serves 8.

▧ Lentil mixture and Sofrito can be made a day ahead.
▧ Storage: Covered, separately, in refrigerator.
▧ Freeze: Not suitable.
▧ Microwave: Not suitable.

BREAM WITH CORIANDER SALSA

4 x 300g whole bream
2 tablespoons olive oil
3 large (750g) tomatoes, peeled, seeded, chopped
2 teaspoons white wine vinegar
2 teaspoons olive oil, extra

CORIANDER SALSA
3 cloves garlic, crushed
3/4 cup firmly packed fresh coriander leaves
1 tablespoon grated lemon rind
2 tablespoons lemon juice
2 teaspoons ground cumin
2 tablespoons tomato paste
1 tablespoon sugar
1/3 cup (80ml) olive oil

1. Cut 3 deep slashes across both sides of each fish; brush fish with half the Coriander Salsa.

2. Heat oil in large pan, cook fish, 1 at a time, until browned both sides and cooked through; brush with remaining Salsa throughout cooking. Serve fish topped with the combined tomatoes, vinegar and extra oil.

3. Coriander Salsa: Blend or process garlic, coriander, rind, juice, cumin, paste and sugar until smooth. Add oil gradually in thin stream, while motor is operating, blend until combined.

Serves 4.

■ Recipe best made just before serving. Coriander Salsa can be made up to 3 days ahead.
■ Storage: Covered, in refrigerator.
■ Freeze: Not suitable.
■ Microwave: Not suitable.

OXTAIL CASSEROLE

¼ cup (60ml) olive oil
2kg chopped oxtail
2 large (400g) onions, sliced
8 cloves garlic, crushed
4 small fresh red chillies, chopped
1 tablespoon ground sweet paprika
1 tablespoon ground cumin
2 teaspoons ground coriander
2 x 425g cans tomatoes
1 medium (200g) red pepper, sliced
¼ cup (60ml) tomato paste
¼ cup chopped fresh oregano leaves
120g quince paste
1 cup (250ml) dry red wine
1 cup (250ml) beef stock

1. Heat oil in large pan, cook oxtail, in batches, stirring, until well browned; drain on absorbent paper.

2. Add onions, garlic, chillies and spices to same pan, cook, stirring, until onions are soft.

3. Return oxtail to pan, add undrained crushed tomatoes and the remaining ingredients, simmer, covered, about 3 hours. Simmer, uncovered, for about 30 minutes or until slightly thickened; cool. Cover, refrigerate 3 hours or overnight. Remove fat from surface of casserole before reheating to serve.

Copper pan from Corso De' Fiori; tiles from Country Floors

Serves 8.
- Best made a day ahead.
- Storage: Covered, in refrigerator.
- Freeze: Suitable.
- Microwave: Not suitable.

TOMATO AND THYME BEEF POT ROAST

**2kg corner fresh beef
 silverside roast**
10 cloves garlic
10 sprigs fresh thyme
2 tablespoons olive oil
425g can tomatoes
1½ cups (375ml) beef stock
¼ cup (60ml) tomato paste
¼ cup (60ml) red wine vinegar
**2 teaspoons chopped fresh
 thyme, extra**
100g quince paste

1. Cut 10 deep slashes in top of beef, insert garlic cloves and thyme sprigs into slashes.

2. Heat oil in large pan; cook beef until well browned all over. Add undrained crushed tomatoes and all remaining ingredients; simmer, covered, for about 2 hours or until beef is tender.

3. Remove beef from pan, cover to keep warm. Boil tomato mixture in pan, uncovered, about 15 minutes or until thickened slightly. Slice beef thinly, serve with tomato mixture.

Serves 8.

▨ Best made just before serving.
▨ Freeze: Not suitable.
▨ Microwave: Not suitable.

ROAST CHICKEN WITH HAM AND OLIVE SEASONING

1.5kg chicken
2 tablespoons brandy
2 tablespoons olive oil
2 cloves garlic, crushed

HAM AND OLIVE SEASONING
1 tablespoon olive oil
1 medium (150g) onion,
    finely chopped
2 cloves garlic, crushed
125g piece double-smoked
    ham, finely chopped
½ cup (35g) stale breadcrumbs
½ cup (60g) seeded black
    olives, chopped
1 tablespoon chopped fresh parsley
1 egg, lightly beaten

1. Fill chicken with Seasoning, secure openings with toothpicks.

2. Tie legs together, tuck wings under, then place chicken, breast side up, on wire rack in baking dish. Brush with some of the combined brandy, oil and garlic. Bake, uncovered, in moderate oven, brushing with brandy mixture occasionally, about 1½ hours or until browned and cooked through.

3. Ham and Olive Seasoning: Heat oil in pan, cook onion and garlic; stirring, until onion is soft. Add ham, breadcrumbs and olives, cook, stirring, 2 minutes. Cool 5 minutes, mix in parsley and egg.

Serves 6.

▓ Best made just before serving.
▓ Freeze: Not suitable.
▓ Microwave: Not suitable.

Tiles and plate from Country Floors; basket from Bondi Storehouse

ACCOMPANIMENTS

As a rule, the Spanish prefer their vegetables cooked, and have developed many unique and delectable dishes that complement both the main ingredient and the course it accompanies. You'll have no problem getting your family to eat their spinach or cauliflower once they taste these appetising and scrumptious recipes.

STUFFED RED AND YELLOW PEPPERS

2 teaspoons olive oil
1 medium (150g) onion, chopped
2 cloves garlic, crushed
1 teaspoon ground sweet paprika
1 teaspoon ground cumin
3/4 cup (150g) long-grain rice
1 cup (250ml) chicken stock
250g minced veal
3 large (270g) egg tomatoes, seeded, chopped
1/3 cup (55g) chopped raisins
1/4 cup (35g) pistachio nuts, toasted, chopped
2 tablespoons tomato paste
2 tablespoons chopped fresh oregano leaves
2 tablespoons chopped fresh parsley
3 medium (600g) red peppers
3 medium (600g) yellow peppers
1 teaspoon olive oil, extra

1. Heat oil in medium heavy-based pan, add onion, garlic and spices; cook, stirring, until onion is soft. Add rice, stir to coat with oil. Add the stock, simmer, covered tightly for 10 minutes. Remove from heat; stand, covered, 10 minutes or until liquid is absorbed. Fluff rice with fork; transfer to large bowl.

2. Add veal to heated medium pan; cook, stirring, until browned.

3. Combine veal, tomatoes, raisins, nuts, paste and herbs with rice mixture.

4. Cut off and reserve tops from peppers; remove and discard seeds and membranes. Place peppers in lightly greased baking dish; divide rice mixture among them, replace the tops. Bake, uncovered, in moderate oven about 35 minutes or until peppers are tender and lightly browned; brush with extra oil.
Serves 6.

■ Filling can be made a day ahead.
■ Storage: Covered, in refrigerator.
■ Freeze: Not suitable.
■ Microwave: Suitable.

FENNEL AND WATERCRESS SALAD

½ medium cos lettuce
1 small (425g) bulb fennel,
   thinly sliced
125g watercress sprigs
2 medium (380g) tomatoes, sliced
1 medium (170g) red onion,
   thinly sliced
½ cup (80g) seeded black olives

LEMON DRESSING
½ cup (125ml) olive oil
¼ cup (60ml) lemon juice
2 cloves garlic, crushed

1. Combine torn lettuce leaves, fennel and watercress in large bowl, with ½ cup (125ml) Lemon Dressing. Top with tomatoes, onion and olives; drizzle with remaining Dressing.

2. Lemon Dressing: Combine all ingredients in jar; shake well.

Serves 4 to 6.

■ Lemon Dressing can be made a day ahead.
■ Storage: Covered, in refrigerator.
■ Freeze: Not suitable.

CAULIFLOWER SALAD

1 medium (1.5kg) cauliflower
½ small (50g) red onion,
    finely chopped
2 eggs
1 tablespoon drained capers
1 tablespoon chopped fresh parsley

CATALAN DRESSING
½ cup (125ml) olive oil
⅓ cup (80ml) red wine vinegar
2 tablespoons lemon juice
2 cloves garlic, crushed
2 teaspoons sugar
1 teaspoon ground sweet paprika
1 teaspoon dried crushed chilli

1. Cut cauliflower into florets, boil, steam or microwave until just tender. Drain, cool 10 minutes.

2. Combine warm cauliflower and onion with Catalan Dressing in large bowl; mix gently. Cover, refrigerate 3 hours or overnight.

3. Place eggs in small pan, cover with cold water, simmer, uncovered, for 8 minutes; rinse under cold water. Shell eggs, push through coarse sieve into small bowl. Top cauliflower mixture with egg, capers and parsley.

Salad platter and bottle from David Jones, Chatswood

Setting from David Jones, Chatswood

4. Catalan Dressing: Combine all ingredients in jar; shake well.

Serves 6.
▨ Best made a day ahead.
▨ Storage: Covered, in refrigerator.
▨ Freeze: Not suitable.
▨ Microwave: Cauliflower suitable.

BEANS WITH CHORIZO AND TOMATOES

2 (340g) chorizo sausages, chopped
8 small (480g) egg tomatoes,
    quartered
1 medium (170g) red onion,
    quartered
2 tablespoons olive oil
2 teaspoons ground sweet paprika
2 teaspoons ground cumin
2 teaspoons sugar
½ teaspoon cracked black pepper
300g green beans, trimmed, halved
300g yellow butter beans,
    trimmed, halved
½ cup (75g) hazelnuts, toasted,
    chopped

PARSLEY OREGANO DRESSING
½ cup (125ml) olive oil
2 cloves garlic, crushed
2 tablespoons white wine vinegar
2 tablespoons chopped
    fresh oregano leaves
2 tablespoons chopped
    fresh parsley

1. Add sausages to medium heated pan, cook, stirring, until browned; drain on absorbent paper.

2. Combine tomatoes, onion, oil, spices, sugar and pepper in medium baking dish. Bake, uncovered, in moderate oven about 30 minutes or until tomatoes are soft. Drain tomatoes and onion into large bowl; reserve pan juices for Parsley Oregano Dressing.

3. Boil, steam or microwave both beans until just tender, then rinse under cold water; drain.

4. Gently toss sausages, tomatoes, onion, both beans, nuts and Dressing together in bowl.

5. Parsley Oregano Dressing: Combine all ingredients with reserved pan juices in jar; shake well.

Serves 6.

■ Can be made 3 hours ahead.
■ Storage: Covered, in refrigerator.
■ Freeze: Not suitable.
■ Microwave: Beans suitable.

Setting and string bag from David Jones, Chatswood

CRUNCHY ASPARAGUS AND KUMARA STICKS

2 bunches (500g) asparagus
1 large (500g) kumara
20g butter
1 tablespoon olive oil
1 clove garlic, crushed
2/3 cup (50g) stale breadcrumbs
1 tablespoon chopped fresh parsley
60g manchego cheese, crumbled

1. Snap off and discard tough ends of asparagus; cut asparagus into 7cm pieces. Peel kumara; cut into approximately 1cm x 7cm pieces. Boil, steam or microwave vegetables, separately, until just tender; drain.

2. Place vegetables in shallow 1.5-litre (6-cup) ovenproof dish; sprinkle with pieces of butter.

3. Heat oil in medium pan, add garlic and breadcrumbs; cook, stirring, until lightly browned. Stir in parsley.

4. Sprinkle breadcrumb mixture over vegetables; top with cheese. Grill until lightly browned.

Serves 6.

■ Best made just before serving.
■ Freeze: Not suitable.
■ Microwave: Vegetables suitable.

Serving platter, bowls and spoon from David Jones, Chatswood

SAFFRON RICE WITH DRIED FRUIT AND NUTS

1½ cups (300g) long-grain rice
2 tablespoons olive oil
20g butter
1 large (200g) onion, chopped
1 cinnamon stick
4 cloves
1 teaspoon saffron threads
1 teaspoon ground coriander
3 strips orange rind
2 cups (500ml) chicken stock
¼ cup (35g) chopped dried apricots
¼ cup (40g) chopped seeded dates
¼ cup (35g) dried currants
¼ cup (40g) pine nuts, toasted
**½ cup (70g) slivered almonds,
     toasted**
**½ cup firmly packed fresh
     coriander leaves**

1. Place rice in medium bowl, cover with cold water, stand for 10 minutes; drain well.

2. Heat oil and butter in large pan, add onion and spices; cook, stirring, until onion is just soft.

3. Add rice and rind, stir until rice is coated with oil. Add stock, simmer, covered tightly, 10 minutes. Remove from heat, stand, covered, about 10 minutes or until liquid is absorbed and rice is tender; discard rind and cinnamon stick. Stir in remaining ingredients.

Serves 4.

■ Best made just before serving.
■ Freeze: Not suitable.
■ Microwave: Not suitable.

SAUTEED SPINACH WITH PROSCIUTTO

1/4 cup (60ml) olive oil
1/4 cup (60ml) lemon juice
2 teaspoons brown sugar
1/2 teaspoon cracked black pepper
1/3 cup (50g) dried currants
1 tablespoon olive oil, extra
1 medium (150g) onion, sliced
4 cloves garlic, crushed
8 slices (120g) prosciutto, chopped
2 teaspoons ground sweet paprika
2 bunches (1kg) English spinach
1/4 cup (40g) pine nuts, toasted

1. Combine oil, juice, sugar, pepper and currants in small bowl; stand 30 minutes.

2. Heat extra oil in medium pan, add onion, garlic, prosciutto and paprika; cook, stirring, until onion is soft.

3. Boil, steam or microwave spinach until just wilted; drain, squeeze out excess liquid.

4. Add spinach, nuts and currant mixture to prosciutto mixture in pan, stir until heated through.

Serves 4 to 6.

▨ Best made just before serving.
▨ Freeze: Not suitable.
▨ Microwave: Spinach suitable.

PISTACHIO QUINCE PASTE

⅓ cup (50g) chopped pistachios,
   toasted
4 lemon zinger tea bags
2½ cups (625ml) boiling water
4 medium (1.3kg) quinces
½ cup (125ml) lemon juice
1 teaspoon ground cloves
4 cups (880g) caster sugar

1. Grease a 23cm round sandwich pan; sprinkle nuts over base.

2. Combine tea bags and water in large bowl, stand 30 minutes. Discard tea bags.

3. Peel, core and roughly chop quinces; combine with tea, juice and cloves in large pan. Simmer, covered, about 45 minutes or until quince is tender. Blend or process quince mixture, in batches, until smooth.

4. Return quince mixture to same pan with sugar, stir over heat, without boiling, until sugar is dissolved. Simmer, uncovered, stirring frequently, about 30 minutes or until very thick and darker in colour. Gently pour quince mixture into prepared pan, stand at room temperature until set.

Makes about 4 cups.

▪ Can be made 3 weeks ahead.
▪ Storage: Covered, in refrigerator.
▪ Freeze: Not suitable.
▪ Microwave: Suitable.

Patterned tiles from Country Floors; shawl from La Campana Spanish Cabaret Restaurant

ROASTED PEPPER AND LIMA BEAN SALAD

1 cup (210g) dried baby lima beans
3 medium (600g) red peppers
2 medium (340g) Lebanese cucumbers, chopped
4 large (360g) egg tomatoes, chopped
1/2 cup (60g) seeded black olives, halved
1 tablespoon chopped fresh oregano leaves

GARLIC CROUTONS
1/2 loaf (300g) unsliced white bread
1/3 cup (80ml) olive oil
2 cloves garlic, crushed

TANGY PAPRIKA DRESSING
1/3 cup (80ml) olive oil
2 tablespoons white wine vinegar
1 tablespoon dry white wine
2 teaspoons ground sweet paprika
1 teaspoon ground coriander
2 cloves garlic, crushed

1. Place beans in medium bowl, cover with cold water, soak overnight. Drain beans, place in pan of boiling water; simmer, uncovered, about 40 minutes or until just tender. Drain, rinse under cold water; cool.

2. Quarter peppers, remove seeds and membranes. Roast under grill or in very hot oven, skin side up, until skin blisters and blackens. Cover pepper in plastic or paper for 5 minutes, peel away skin; slice peppers into 1cm pieces.

3. Combine beans, peppers and remaining ingredients with Croutons in bowl; toss with Tangy Paprika Dressing.

4. Garlic Croutons: Remove crusts from bread. Cut bread into 2cm cubes, toss with oil and garlic in medium bowl. Place croutons on oven tray, bake in moderate oven about 15 minutes or until lightly browned and crisp.

Tangy Paprika Dressing: Combine all ingredients in jar, shake well.

Serves 6.

▨ Lima beans can be cooked a day ahead. Croutons and Tangy Paprika Dressing can be made a day ahead.
▨ Storage: Croutons, in airtight container. Beans and Dressing, covered, separately, in refrigerator.
▨ Freeze: Not suitable.
▨ Microwave: Beans suitable.

CRUSTY BREAD ROLLS

2 teaspoons (7g) dried yeast
1 teaspoon sugar
½ cup (125ml) warm milk
1 cup (250ml) warm water,
**   approximately**
4 cups (600g) plain flour
1 teaspoon salt
2 tablespoons olive oil
1 tablespoon cornmeal
2 teaspoons plain flour, extra

1. Combine yeast, sugar, milk and water in small bowl. Cover, stand in warm place about 10 minutes or until frothy.

2. Sift flour and salt into large bowl, add combined yeast mixture and oil; mix to a soft dough.

3. Knead dough on floured surface about 10 minutes or until smooth and elastic. Place dough in oiled bowl, cover tightly, stand in warm place about 30 minutes or until doubled in size.

4. Turn dough onto floured surface, knead until smooth. Divide dough into 8 pieces. Shape each piece into a ball, place on greased oven trays. Cover loosely with a tea towel, stand in warm place about 20 minutes or until doubled in size. Brush rolls with a little extra milk; sprinkle with combined cornmeal and extra flour. Place rolls in cold oven, turn to moderately hot, bake about 25 minutes or until rolls are browned and sound hollow when tapped.

Makes 8.

■ Best made on day of serving.
■ Storage: In airtight container.
■ Freeze: Suitable.
■ Microwave: Not suitable.

Glasses from David Jones, Chatswood

2. Heat oil in large pan, cook potatoes, stirring occasionally, until browned and crisp. Add bacon and garlic, cook, stirring occasionally, until bacon is crisp. Remove from pan, cover to keep warm.

3. Add apple, cabbage, vinegar, juice and sugar to same pan; cook, stirring, about 5 minutes or until apple is almost tender. Return potato mixture to pan, gently mix in remaining ingredients.

Serves 6.

■ Best made just before serving.
■ Freeze: Not suitable.
■ Microwave: Potatoes suitable.

RED CABBAGE, POTATO AND BACON SALAD

5 medium (1kg) potatoes, chopped
2 tablespoons olive oil
4 bacon rashers, chopped
4 cloves garlic, crushed
1 medium (150g) apple,
   thinly sliced
½ medium (750g) red
   cabbage, shredded
¼ cup (60ml) red wine vinegar
2 tablespoons lemon juice
1 tablespoon sugar
½ cup (85g) raisins
¼ cup (40g) pine nuts, toasted
¼ cup chopped fresh mint

1. Boil, steam or microwave potatoes until just tender; drain, spread out on absorbent paper to dry.

SCALLOPED POTATO AND LEEK CASSEROLE

5 large (1.5kg) potatoes,
  thinly sliced
1 medium (350g) leek, chopped
3 teaspoons chopped fresh
  thyme leaves
¼ cup (60ml) chicken stock
¼ cup (60ml) dry white wine
1 tablespoon olive oil
1 clove garlic, crushed

1. Layer half the potatoes in a deep 3.5-litre (14-cup) greased ovenproof dish; top with leek and half the thyme. Repeat layering with remaining potatoes and thyme.

2. Combine remaining ingredients in jug; pour over potatoes. Bake, covered, in moderate oven 45 minutes; uncover, bake another 45 minutes until browned.

Serves 6
■ Best made just before serving.
■ Freeze: Not suitable.
■ Microwave: Not suitable.

CHAR-GRILLED VEGETABLES IN MINTY VINAIGRETTE

3 medium (600g) red peppers
3 medium (360g) green zucchini
3 medium (360g) yellow zucchini
4 (240g) baby eggplants
2 tablespoons olive oil
250g cherry tomatoes, halved

MINTY VINAIGRETTE
2 cloves garlic, crushed
2 teaspoons cumin seeds, toasted
½ cup (125ml) olive oil
1 tablespoon lemon juice
2 tablespoons red wine vinegar
1 tablespoon shredded fresh mint

2. Cut zucchini and eggplants lengthways into 1cm slices. Heat oil in griddle pan (or grill or barbecue), cook zucchini and eggplants in batches until charred and cooked through; remove from pan. Add tomatoes to same pan, cook until just softened. Serve immediately, drizzled with Minty Vinaigrette.

1. Quarter peppers, remove seeds and membranes. Roast under grill or in very hot oven, skin side up, until skin blisters and blackens. Cover pepper pieces in plastic or paper for 5 minutes, then peel away skin, slice peppers thickly.

3. Minty Vinaigrette: Combine all ingredients in jar; shake well.

Serves 4.

- Vegetables best prepared just before serving. Minty Vinaigrette can be made a day ahead.
- Storage: Covered, in refrigerator.
- Freeze: Not suitable.
- Microwave: Not suitable.

Plate from Accoutrement; throw rug from Corso De' Fiori

GARLIC, VEGETABLE AND RICE CASSEROLE

1 bulb (70g) garlic
2 tablespoons olive oil
1 medium (150g) onion, sliced
1 medium (200g) red pepper, sliced
1 medium (200g) green
    pepper, sliced
4 medium (760g) tomatoes,
    peeled, sliced
125g green beans, trimmed, halved
2 small (120g) baby
    eggplants, sliced
¼ cup (35g) dried currants
1 teaspoon ground sweet paprika
1½ cups (300g) long-grain rice
3 cups (750ml) boiling
    chicken stock

1. Place unpeeled garlic bulb on oven tray, brush with a little of the oil; bake, uncovered, in moderately hot oven about 30 minutes or until slightly soft. Heat remaining oil in large flameproof baking dish; add onion, peppers, tomatoes, beans and eggplants. Cook, stirring, about 10 minutes or until vegetables are just soft. Stir in currants and paprika.

2. Sprinkle rice over vegetables; pour stock over rice. Place garlic bulb in the centre of mixture; bake, uncovered, in moderately hot oven about 30 minutes, stirring halfway through cooking time, or until rice is just tender.

Serves 4 to 6.

■ Best made just before serving.
■ Freeze: Not suitable.
■ Microwave: Not suitable.

Place setting from David Jones, Chatswood

POTATO SALAD WITH GHERKIN AND RED PEPPER

7 medium (1.4kg) potatoes,
    unpeeled, quartered
1 large (300g) red onion, sliced
1 cup (180g) seeded green olives
3/4 cup (100g) small gherkins
1 medium (200g) red pepper,
    chopped

HERB DRESSING
1/3 cup (80ml) olive oil
1/4 cup (60ml) lemon juice
2 tablespoons red wine vinegar
2 tablespoons fresh mint leaves
2 tablespoons fresh oregano leaves
2 cloves garlic, crushed

1. Boil, steam or microwave potatoes until just tender. Drain potatoes, spread out on absorbent paper to dry.

2. Combine potatoes with remaining ingredients and Herb Dressing in large bowl just before serving.

3. Herb Dressing: Combine all ingredients in jar; shake well.

Serves 6 to 8.

■ Potato Salad and Herb Dressing can be made 3 hours ahead.
■ Storage: Covered, separately, in refrigerator.
■ Freeze: Not suitable.
■ Microwave: Suitable.

WARM ONION AND MIXED PEPPER SALAD

3 medium (600g) red peppers
2 medium (400g) yellow peppers
¼ cup (60ml) olive oil
3 medium (450g) onions,
    thickly sliced
¼ cup (55g) sugar
⅓ cup (80ml) chicken stock
2 tablespoons lemon juice
¼ cup (40g) pine nuts, toasted
¼ cup (35g) slivered
    almonds, toasted
½ cup fresh flat-leaf parsley,
    roughly chopped

1. Quarter peppers, remove seeds and membranes. Roast under grill or in very hot oven, skin side up, until skin blisters and blackens. Cover pepper pieces in plastic or paper for 5 minutes, then peel away skin, slice peppers thickly.

2. Heat oil in large pan, add onions, cook, stirring, about 5 minutes or until lightly browned. Stir in sugar and stock, cook, stirring, about 5 minutes or until golden brown.

3. Add peppers, juice and nuts, stir until heated through. Stir in parsley just before serving.

Serves 4.

- Peppers can be prepared 3 hours ahead.
- Storage: Covered, in refrigerator.
- Freeze: Not suitable.
- Microwave: Not suitable.

VALENCIAN SALAD

6 large (1.8kg) oranges
2 medium (380g) tomatoes
1 large (300g) red onion, sliced
1 cup (150g) manchego cheese, chopped
¾ cup (120g) seeded black olives
2 large (640g) avocados, chopped

ORANGE MINT DRESSING
2 tablespoons olive oil
2 tablespoons red wine vinegar
2 tablespoons orange juice
1 clove garlic, crushed
1 tablespoon chopped fresh mint

1. Peel oranges thickly, cut between membranes into segments. Quarter tomatoes, remove seeds; cut quarters in half lengthways.

2. Combine orange segments and tomato pieces with remaining ingredients and Dressing in large bowl; toss gently.

3. Orange Mint Dressing: Combine all ingredients in jar; shake well.

Serves 6 to 8.

■ Salad best assembled just before serving. Orange Mint Dressing can be made a day ahead.
■ Storage: Covered, in refrigerator.
■ Freeze: Not suitable.

Salad bowl, plates and napkins from David Jones, Chatswood; salad servers from Kitchen Kapers; basket from Shack

SWEETS & DRINKS

The Spanish have a sweet-tooth not unlike our own, and love to end a meal with something rich and preferably sticky. Caramel and honey in custards, rice and nuts in puddings, and nougat on its own dominate desserts, while hot chocolate and sangria vie for honours as the favourite drink.

BAKED ORANGE CARAMEL CUSTARD

½ cup (125ml) water
¾ cup (165g) caster sugar
4 eggs
4 egg yolks
⅓ cup (75g) caster sugar, extra
1 teaspoon grated orange rind
2 teaspoons Grand Marnier
2 teaspoons vanilla essence
1 cup (250ml) milk
1 cup (250ml) cream

1. Combine water and sugar in small heavy-based pan, stir over heat, without boiling, until sugar is dissolved. Boil, without stirring, about 10 minutes or until browned.

2. Pour caramel over base of lightly oiled 20cm ring pan.

3. Combine eggs, yolks, extra sugar, rind, liqueur and essence in medium bowl, whisk until combined. Combine milk and cream in small pan, stir over heat until mixture almost boils. Remove from heat; stand 5 minutes. Gradually whisk hot milk mixture into egg mixture; strain into jug, gradually pour into prepared ring pan.

4. Place pan in baking dish with enough boiling water to come halfway up sides of pan. Bake in moderately slow oven, about 35 minutes or until custard is just set. Remove pan from water, cool. Cover, refrigerate overnight. Run knife around edge of custard, carefully turn custard onto large rimmed plate.

Serves 6.

■ Must be made a day ahead.
■ Storage: Covered, in refrigerator.
■ Freeze: Not suitable.
■ Microwave: Not suitable.

FRIED MILK

Leche frita (or fried milk in English) are delicious deep-fried custard shapes.

2½ cups (625ml) milk
1 cinnamon stick
2cm x 8cm strip orange rind
2 eggs
1 egg yolk
⅓ cup (50g) plain flour
¼ cup (35g) cornflour
1 teaspoon vanilla essence
½ cup (110g) caster sugar
plain flour, extra
vegetable oil, for deep-frying
½ cup (110g) caster sugar, extra
½ teaspoon ground cinnamon

1. Grease 20cm x 30cm lamington pan. Cover base with baking paper, which extends over the 2 long sides. Combine the milk, cinnamon stick and rind in medium pan, bring to boil, remove from heat; cover, stand 10 minutes. Discard cinnamon stick and rind.

2. Whisk eggs, yolk, flours, essence and sugar together in medium bowl until smooth.

3. Whisk egg mixture gradually into warm milk mixture, stir, over heat, until custard boils and thickens. Simmer, stirring, about 2 minutes or until custard starts to leave side of the pan. Spread mixture into prepared pan; cool. Cover, refrigerate about 2 hours or until firm.

4. Turn custard out; cut into a variety of shapes.

5. Dust custard shapes with extra flour; deep-fry in hot oil, in batches, until browned. Drain on absorbent paper for a few minutes until cool enough to handle.

6. Gently toss hot custard shapes in combined extra sugar and cinnamon; serve immediately.

Makes about 20.

- Can be prepared a day ahead. Deep-fry custard shapes just before serving.
- Storage: Covered, in refrigerator.
- Freeze: Not suitable.
- Microwave: Not suitable.

Plates from Accoutrement

HONEY-WINE PASTRIES

We used a Sauternes-style dessert wine for this recipe.

2 cups (300g) plain flour
1/2 teaspoon ground cinnamon
**1/2 teaspoon finely grated
   lemon rind**
1/3 cup (80ml) light olive oil
2/3 cup (160ml) sweet dessert wine
vegetable oil, for deep-frying
icing sugar mixture
1/2 cup (125ml) honey
1/2 teaspoon whole cloves
1 cinnamon stick
2 star anise

1. Sift flour and ground cinnamon into medium bowl; mix in rind, oil and wine to form a soft dough. Knead dough on floured surface until smooth. Cover with plastic wrap; stand 30 minutes.

2. Divide pastry in half; roll each piece between sheets of baking paper until 5mm thick. Cut into 5cm squares; re-roll pastry scraps, resting the pastry between each rolling.

3. Deep-fry pastries in hot oil, in batches, until browned; drain on absorbent paper. Dust with sifted icing sugar.

4. Meanwhile, combine honey, cloves, cinnamon stick and star anise in pan. Boil, uncovered, 2 minutes; strain into a jug, discard spices. Cool honey syrup 5 minutes. Transfer pastries to plate, then drizzle syrup over pastries.

Makes about 36 pastries.

■ Pastry squares best deep-fried just before serving. Syrup can be prepared a day ahead.
■ Storage: Covered, in refrigerator.
■ Freeze: Not suitable.
■ Microwave: Syrup suitable.

SANGRIA PUNCH

We used a pinot noir-style red wine in this special version of the traditional recipe.

6 whole cloves
1 cinnamon stick
¼ cup (55g) caster sugar
3 cups (750ml) orange juice
½ cup (125ml) port
10cm thin strip orange rind
750ml bottle light red wine
½ cup (125ml) brandy
½ cup (125ml) gin
½ cup (125ml) vermouth
⅓ cup (80ml) grenadine
1.25litre bottle lemonade
1 large (300g) orange, quartered, sliced
1 large (200g) red apple, quartered, cored, sliced

1. Combine spices, sugar, juice, port and rind in medium pan; stir over heat, without boiling, until sugar is dissolved. Simmer, uncovered, 5 minutes, strain into a large bowl; cool.

2. Add alcohol, grenadine, lemonade and orange to juice mixture; cover, refrigerate 3 hours or overnight. Add apple just before serving.

Makes 3.5 litres.

▧ Best made a day ahead.
▧ Storage: Covered, in refrigerator.
▧ Freeze: Not suitable.
▧ Microwave: Not suitable.

113

CATALAN CINNAMON CUSTARD

A Spanish version of creme brulee.

600ml cream
1/4 cup (60ml) milk
3 cinnamon sticks, halved
3 strips lemon rind
5 egg yolks
1 egg
1/3 cup (75g) caster sugar
1/4 teaspoon ground cinnamon
1 tablespoon pure icing sugar
1 1/2 tablespoons brown sugar

1. Place cream, milk, cinnamon sticks and rind in medium pan, stir over heat until mixture just comes to the boil. Remove from heat, stand 5 minutes, strain into jug; discard cinnamon sticks and rind.

2. Whisk yolks, egg and caster sugar in medium bowl until pale and thick; gradually whisk in hot cream mixture.

3. Place 6 x 1/2 cup (125ml) ovenproof dishes in baking dish; divide custard mixture among dishes. Pour enough boiling water into baking dish to come halfway up sides of dishes. Bake, uncovered, in moderately slow oven, about 35 minutes or until set. Remove dishes from water, cool. Cover; refrigerate 3 hours or overnight.

4. Push ground cinnamon, icing and brown sugars through fine sieve, then sprinkle evenly over custards. Cover, refrigerate 1 hour. Spray custards lightly with water, cook under very hot grill about 2 minutes or until top is caramelised. Refrigerate about 10 minutes or until top sets.

Serves 6.

■ Custards, without sugar top, can be made 2 days ahead.
■ Storage: Covered, in refrigerator.
■ Freeze: Not suitable.
■ Microwave: Not suitable.

Rug and sunflower plate from Sirocco Homewares; spoon from Kitchen Kapers

TURRON

Turron, a nougat-like sweet containing almonds and honey, is traditionally made at Christmas in Spain.

8 x 15.5cm x 20cm sheets rice paper
²/₃ cup (160ml) honey
¹/₃ cup (80ml) syrup glucose
¹/₄ cup (60ml) water
1¹/₄ cups (275g) caster sugar
2 egg whites
4 cups (640g) blanched almonds, toasted
2 teaspoons finely grated lemon rind

Tiles from Country Floors

1. Grease 2 x 20cm x 30cm lamington pans; trim 4 sheets of rice paper to cover bases of pans. Trim 2 sheets of foil to fit tops of prepared pans. Grease 1 side of each piece of foil well.

2. Combine honey, glucose, water and sugar in medium pan; stir over heat, without boiling, until sugar is dissolved. Bring to boil; boil rapidly, without stirring, about 10 minutes or until syrup reaches 154°C (crack stage) when measured with a candy thermometer, or when a teaspoon of syrup, dropped into a cup of cold water, forms brittle threads. Remove from heat.

3. Meanwhile, beat egg whites in small bowl with electric mixer until firm peaks form. Transfer egg whites to large bowl; with mixer operating, add hot syrup mixture in a thin, steady stream. Beat about 3 minutes or until mixture is very thick and holds its shape.

4. Working quickly, stir in nuts and rind then divide mixture between prepared pans. Press sheets of prepared foil over top, smooth surface; remove foil. Trim remaining sheets of rice paper to fit tops then press over the surface of Turron. Cool to room temperature (about 4 hours). Turn Turron onto board. Using an oiled knife, trim edges. Cut into 4cm squares.

Makes about 50.

■ Can be made 2 days ahead.
■ Storage: Airtight container in a cool, dry place.
▨ Freeze: Not suitable.
▨ Microwave: Not suitable.

ALMOND RICE PUDDING WITH POACHED PEARS

2 cups (500ml) milk
1 tablespoon grated lemon rind
1 cinnamon stick
½ cup (100g) calrose rice
⅓ cup (40g) ground almonds
1 cup (250ml) cream
2 teaspoons gelatine
1 tablespoon water
⅓ cup (75g) sugar
2 egg whites

POACHED PEARS
2 medium (460g) firm
   pears, peeled
1 medium (140g) lemon, sliced
¾ cup (180ml) sweet sherry
¾ cup (180ml) dry red wine
½ cup (110g) sugar
2 cinnamon sticks

3. Sprinkle gelatine over water in cup, stand in small pan of simmering water; stir until dissolved. Stir gelatine mixture and sugar into rice mixture; cool. Discard cinnamon stick.

4. Beat egg whites in small bowl with electric mixer until soft peaks form; fold into rice mixture in 2 batches. Spoon rice mixture into prepared dishes. Cover, refrigerate until firm. Serve Puddings with Poached Pears.

1. Lightly oil 6 x ⅔ cup (160ml) oven-proof dishes. Combine milk, rind and cinnamon in medium pan, bring to boil; gradually stir in rice. Cover with tight-fitting lid, simmer about 15 minutes or until rice is just tender.

2. Add almonds and cream; cook, stirring, about 10 minutes or until rice is very tender and mixture thickens.

5. Poached Pears: Cut each pear into 8 wedges, discard cores. Combine pears and remaining ingredients in medium pan, stir over heat, without boiling, until sugar is dissolved. Simmer, uncovered, about 15 minutes or until pears are tender and syrup thickens slightly.

Serves 6.

▪ Can be made a day ahead.
▪ Storage: Covered, separately, in refrigerator.
▪ Freeze: Not suitable.
▪ Microwave: Not suitable.

Tiles from Country Floors

2. Pour 2 tablespoons of batter in heated greased heavy-based pan; cook until lightly browned, turn pancake, brown other side. Repeat with remaining batter. Serve pancakes with Almond Cream, sprinkled with nuts and dusted with sifted icing sugar.

3. Almond Cream: Beat cream cheese and icing sugar in small bowl with electric mixer until smooth; stir in Madeira and nuts. Beat cream in small bowl until soft peaks form, fold into cheese mixture.

Serves 6.

- Unfilled pancakes can be made a day ahead. Almond Cream best made on day of serving.
- Storage: Pancakes, in airtight container. Almond Cream, covered, in refrigerator.
- Freeze: Unfilled pancakes suitable.
- Microwave: Not suitable.

PANCAKES WITH ALMOND CREAM

3/4 cup (110g) plain flour
2 teaspoons caster sugar
3 eggs, lightly beaten
30g butter, melted
1 cup (250ml) milk
2 tablespoons flaked
    almonds, toasted
icing sugar mixture

ALMOND CREAM
150g packaged cream cheese
1/3 cup (55g) icing sugar mixture
2 tablespoons Madeira
1/4 cup (20g) flaked
    almonds, toasted
300ml thickened cream

1. Sift flour and sugar into medium bowl, gradually whisk in combined eggs, butter and milk until smooth. Cover, stand 1 hour.

HOT CHOCOLATE DRINK

3½ cups (875ml) milk
½ cup (125ml) cream
200g dark chocolate, chopped
6 cinnamon sticks

1. Combine milk and cream in medium pan, stir over heat until almost boiling. Remove from heat, add chocolate; whisk until chocolate is melted and mixture is smooth. Serve with cinnamon sticks.

Serves 6.

▨ Best made just before serving.
▨ Freeze: Not suitable.
▨ Microwave: Suitable.

Tiles from Bisanna Tiles

CHOCOLATE AND CINNAMON ICE-CREAM

We used Lindt bittersweet chocolate, sold in 85g packets.

2 cups (500ml) milk
3 cinnamon sticks, halved
170g bittersweet chocolate, finely chopped
8 egg yolks
½ cup (110g) caster sugar
300ml thickened cream

1. Place milk, cinnamon sticks and chocolate in large heavy-based pan. Stir over low heat until chocolate is melted. Remove from heat, stand 5 minutes, strain into jug; discard cinnamon sticks.

2. Beat egg yolks and sugar in small bowl with electric mixer until thick and pale. Gradually add hot chocolate mixture to egg yolk mixture while motor is operating; beat until just combined.

3. Return mixture to same pan, stir over heat, without boiling, for about 15 minutes or until mixture thickens slightly. Remove from heat, transfer to large bowl; cover, cool. Refrigerate about 1 hour or until cold. Stir in cream then pour mixture into 14cm x 21cm loaf pan; cover with foil, freeze several hours or until just firm.

4. Beat ice-cream in large bowl with electric mixer until smooth. Return ice-cream to same pan; cover with foil, freeze until firm.

Serves 6 to 8.

- Can be made 2 days ahead.
- Storage: Covered, in freezer.
- Microwave: Not suitable.

Tiles from Bisanna Tiles

FIGS IN RED WINE WITH SPICED CREAM

30 (700g) whole dried figs
4 thin strips orange rind
2 cinnamon sticks
1 cup (220g) caster sugar
1/4 cup (60ml) Grand Marnier
1 cup (250ml) orange juice
1 cup (250ml) dry red wine
1½ cups (375ml) port
2 tablespoons flaked
    almonds, toasted

ALMOND CINNAMON SUGAR
½ teaspoon ground cinnamon
½ teaspoon ground cloves
1½ tablespoons caster sugar
2 tablespoons flaked almonds,
    toasted, crushed

SPICED CREAM
300ml thickened cream
1 tablespoon honey
½ teaspoon ground cinnamon
1/3 cup (80ml) sour cream

1. Holding stem, stretch and reshape each fig into a round. Make a small cut in base of fig, fill with Almond Cinnamon Sugar, gently squeeze base to enclose filling completely.

2. Combine rind, cinnamon sticks, sugar, liqueur, juice, wine and port in large pan. Stir over heat, without boiling, until sugar is dissolved. Simmer, uncovered, about 7 minutes or until slightly thickened.

3. Add figs to syrup, simmer, stirring occasionally, about 15 minutes or until figs are soft and syrup has thickened. Discard rind and cinnamon sticks. Serve figs warm, with syrup, Spiced Cream and nuts.

4. Almond Cinnamon Sugar: Combine all ingredients in small bowl.

5. Spiced Cream: Beat thickened cream, honey and cinnamon in small bowl until firm peaks form; fold in sour cream.

Serves 8 to 10.

■ Syrup can be made a day ahead.
■ Storage: Covered, in refrigerator.
■ Freeze: Not suitable.
■ Microwave: Not suitable.

Saffron threads

Saffron powder

Bird's-eye chillies

Star anise

GLOSSARY

Here are some terms, names and alternatives to help everyone use and understand our recipes perfectly.

ALMONDS:

Blanched: skins removed.

Flaked: cut in paper-thin slices.

Ground: we used packaged commercially ground nuts.

Slivered: small lengthways-cut pieces.

BACON RASHERS: slices of bacon.

BAY LEAVES: aromatic leaves from the bay tree.

BEANS:

Haricot: small, white beans; require soaking. Also known as navy beans.

Lima: kidney-shaped, cream-coloured dried beans; require soaking. Also known as butter beans.

BEEF:

Corner of fresh silverside: boneless cut, from the thigh.

Yellow pepper

Spanish red pepper

Red pepper

Green pepper

BREADCRUMBS:

Packaged: use fine packaged breadcrumbs.

Stale: use 1- or 2-day-old bread made into crumbs by grating, blending or processing.

BUTTER: use salted or unsalted (also called sweet) butter if neither is specified; 125g is equal to 1 stick butter.

CAYENNE PEPPER: another name for chilli pepper; most often used dried then ground.

CHEESE:

Cream: commonly known as "Philadelphia" or "Philly"; a soft cows' milk cheese having no less than 33% butterfat.

Goats' cheese: made from goats' milk, has an earthy, strong taste; available in both soft and firm textures.

Manchego: an aged, semi-firm, intensely flavoured Spanish cheese made from sheeps' milk. Available from specialty cheese stores; substitute haloumi or fetta if not readily available.

Soft blue vein: creamy, sweet rather than acidic, double-cream blue cheese; blue castello is an example.

CHICKPEAS: garbanzos. Available dried or canned.

CHILLIES: available in many different types and sizes. Wash hands with warm soapy water immediately after seeding, deveining or chopping fresh chillies because they can burn your skin.

Dried crushed: available from supermarkets and Asian food stores.

Powder: the Asian variety is the hottest, made from ground chillies; it can be used as a substitute for fresh chillies in the proportion of 1/2 teaspoon ground chilli powder to 1 medium chopped fresh chilli.

CHOCOLATE:

Bittersweet: good quality eating chocolate with a low sugar content. We used the Lindt brand.

Dark: eating chocolate.

CLAMS: we used a small ridge-shelled variety of this bivalve mollusc; also known as vongole.

CORIANDER: also known as cilantro or Chinese parsley.

CORNFLOUR: cornstarch.

CORNMEAL: ground dried corn (maize); similar to polenta but slightly coarser. One can be substituted for the other, but textures will vary.

CREAM: fresh pouring cream with a minimum 35% fat content.

Sour: a thick, commercially cultured soured cream containing not less than 35% fat.

Thickened: whipping. Minimum fat content 35%; contains a thickening agent.

CUMIN: available ground or in seed form. To toast seeds, place in dry pan, cook, stirring until fragrant.

EGGPLANT: aubergine.

Thyme

Pomegranate

Quince

Flat-leaf parsley

Coriander

Curly parsley

Marjoram

Mint

Oregano

Basil

EMPANADILLAS: small version of an empanada, a turnover filled with meat.

ENGLISH SPINACH: a soft-leaved vegetable; young silverbeet or Swiss chard can be substituted.

ESSENCE: extract.

FENNEL: also known as finocchio or anise. Tasting of aniseed, the bulb can be eaten raw or cooked and the feathery leaves used as a herb.

FISH FILLETS: fish pieces that have been boned and skinned.

FLOUR:

Plain: all-purpose.

Self-raising: substitute plain (all-purpose) flour and baking powder in the proportions of 1 cup (150g) plain flour to 2 level teaspoons baking powder. Sift together several times before using.

FRESH HERBS: we have specified when to use fresh or dried herbs. We used dried (not ground) herbs in the proportion of 1:4 for fresh herbs: use 1 teaspoon dried herbs instead of 4 teaspoons (1 tablespoon) chopped fresh herbs.

GHERKIN: cornichon.

GLOBE ARTICHOKE: large flower-bud of a member of the thistle family; having tough petal-like leaves, edible when cooked.

GLUCOSE SYRUP (liquid glucose): made from wheat starch.

GRAND MARNIER: orange-flavoured liqueur based on Cognac-brandy.

GRENADINE: a non-alcoholic syrup made from pomegranate juice; bright red in colour, it's used to colour and flavour drinks and desserts. Imitation cordial is also available.

GUAVA PASTE: made from guava pulp and sugar, cooked to a paste-like consistency. Available in cans from delicatessens and specialty stores.

KUMARA: orange-fleshed sweet potato.

LAMB:

Drumsticks: also known as Frenched shanks and trimmed shanks, these are lamb shanks with the gristle that's attached at the narrow end of the bone removed and the bone trimmed.

Fillet: tenderloin; the smaller piece of meat from a row of loin chops or cutlets.

Kidney: lamb kidneys have only 1 lobe. Remove any surface membrane and fat before using.

Leg: from the hindquarter.

Loin: row of eight ribs from the tender mid-section.

Minced: ground lamb.

LEBANESE CUCUMBER: thin-skinned variety also known as the European or burpless cucumber.

LEMONADE: a carbonated soft drink such as 7UP.

LEMON ZINGER TEA BAGS: a herbal tea consisting of hibiscus flowers, rosehips, roasted chicory root, orange peel, lemon grass, lemon peel, whole dried lemons, natural lemon flavour and citric acid.

MADEIRA: a dessert wine, fortified with brandy.

MILK: we used full-cream homogenised milk unless otherwise specified.

Rosemary

Tarragon

123

Globe artichoke

Fennel

English spinach

Lebanese cucumber

Green onion

Spring onion

French shallot

Red onion

OIL:

Light olive: a mild-flavoured olive oil.

Olive: a blend of refined and virgin olive oils, good for everyday cooking.

Vegetable: we used a polyunsaturated vegetable oil.

ONIONS:

Green: also called scallions, spring onions or shallots; have long green tops and very small white bulbs.

Red: also known as Spanish, Bermuda or purple.

Spring: have crisp, narrow green-leafed tops and a fairly large sweet white bulb.

PAPRIKA: ground dried red peppers; we used both Spanish sweet and hot paprikas in this book, available from delicatessens and specialty stores.

PEPPERS: capsicum or bell peppers; remove seeds and membranes before using.

Spanish red: a sweet, elongated pepper also known as a pimiento.

PINOT NOIR: a light style of red wine.

PIPIS: small smooth-shelled triangular shaped bivalve mollusc.

POMEGRANATE: round juicy fruit, the size of a large orange, with leathery red skin. Contains white seeds in pinkish-red flesh.

PORT: a rich, sweet dessert wine fortified with brandy.

PRAWNS: shrimp.

PROSCIUTTO: an air-dried, unsmoked, salt-cured ham; ready to eat without cooking.

QUAIL: small game birds ranging in weight from 250g to 300g; also known as partridge.

QUINCE: yellow-skinned fruit with hard texture and astringent, tart taste; eaten cooked.

Paste: called membrillo in Spain; quince and sugar cooked down to a paste-like consistency. Available from delicatessens and specialty stores.

RAISINS: dried dark grapes.

RICE:

Calrose: a medium-grained variety readily available and used for most of the rice-based recipes in this book.

Long-grain: elongated grain, remains separate when cooked.

Short-grain: fat, almost round grain with a high starch content; tends to clump together when cooked.

RICE PAPER: an edible paper used as a wrapper or to line pans; available from specialty food shops and Asian suppliers.

RIND: zest.

SAFFRON: available in strands or ground form. Quality varies greatly; the best can be quite expensive. Store in the freezer.

SAUSAGES:

Blood: also known as blood pudding; made with pork blood and fat, mildly spiced.

Chorizo: spicy; made from pork, garlic and red peppers.

SCALLOPS: a mollusc; we used scallops with coral (roe) attached.

SCORE: to cut shallow slashes in certain foods, particularly meat or seafood, to permeate flavours, to ensure even cooking and as a decoration.

SHALLOTS: small, brown French onions; the name is frequently incorrectly attached to the green onion.

SOFRITO: one of the classic Spanish sauces; made with onions cooked slowly with tomatoes to a jam-like consistency.

SPATCHCOCK: a small chicken (poussin), no more than 6 weeks old, weighing a maximum 500g. Also a technique where a small chicken is split open, then flattened and grilled.

STAR ANISE: the dried star-shaped fruit of an evergreen tree having a slightly bitter aniseed flavour.

STELLINE: tiny star-shaped pasta frequently used in soups and stews.

SUGAR: we used coarse granulated table sugar, also known as crystal sugar, unless otherwise specified.

Brown: a soft, fine granulated sugar containing molasses which gives it its characteristic colour.

Caster: also known as superfine or finely granulated table sugar.

Icing sugar mixture: also known as confectioners' sugar or powdered sugar, with the addition of cornflour.

Pure icing: also known as confectioners' sugar or powdered sugar.

VEAL: meat from a young calf, identified by its creamy pink flesh, fine texture and delicate taste.

Medallions: small, coin-sized pieces cut from the nut (round) of veal.

Minced: ground veal.

VERMOUTH: a wine flavoured with a number of different herbs, mostly used as an aperitif and for cocktails.

VINEGAR:

Red wine: based on fermented red wine.

White wine: based on fermented white wine.

YEAST: allow 2 teaspoons (7g) dried yeast to 15g compressed yeast; a ¼oz packet is equal to 7g.

ZUCCHINI: courgette.

MAKE YOUR OWN STOCK

If you prefer to make your own stock, these recipes can be made up to 4 days ahead and stored, covered, in the refrigerator. Be sure to remove any fat from the surface after the cooled stock has been refrigerated overnight. If the stock is to be kept longer, it is best to freeze it in smaller quantities. Stock is also available in cans or tetra packs. Stock cubes or powder can be used. As a guide, 1 teaspoon of stock powder or 1 small crumbled stock cube mixed with 1 cup (250ml) water will give a fairly strong stock. Be aware of the salt and fat content of cubes, powders and prepared stocks.

BEEF STOCK

2kg meaty beef bones
2 medium (300g) onions
2 sticks celery, chopped
2 medium (250g) carrots, chopped
3 bay leaves
2 teaspoons black peppercorns
5 litres (20 cups) water
3 litres (12 cups) water, extra

Place bones and unpeeled chopped onions in baking dish. Bake in hot oven about 1 hour or until bones and onions are well browned. Transfer bones and onions to large pan, add celery, carrots, bay leaves, peppercorns and water, simmer, uncovered, 3 hours. Add extra water, simmer, uncovered, further 1 hour; strain into large bowl.

CHICKEN STOCK

2kg chicken bones
2 medium (300g) onions, chopped
2 sticks celery, chopped
2 medium (250g) carrots, chopped
3 bay leaves
2 teaspoons black peppercorns
5 litres (20 cups) water

Combine all ingredients in large pan, simmer, uncovered, 2 hours; strain into large bowl.

FISH STOCK

1.5kg fish bones
3 litres (12 cups) water
1 medium (150g) onion, chopped
2 sticks celery, chopped
2 bay leaves
1 teaspoon black peppercorns

Combine all ingredients in large pan, simmer, uncovered, 20 minutes; strain into large bowl.

VEGETABLE STOCK

2 large (360g) carrots, chopped
2 large (360g) parsnips, chopped
4 medium (600g) onions, chopped
12 sticks celery, chopped
4 bay leaves
2 teaspoons black peppercorns
6 litres (24 cups) water

Combine all ingredients in large pan, simmer, uncovered, 1½ hours; strain into large bowl.

All stock recipes make about 2.5 litres (10 cups).

Calrose rice

Long-grain rice

Short-grain rice

Kumara

Finger eggplant

Eggplant

INDEX

QUICK CONVERSION GUIDE

Wherever you live in the world you can use our recipes with the help of our easy-to-follow conversions for all your cooking needs. These conversions are approximate only. The difference between the exact and approximate conversion of liquid and dry measures amounts to only a teaspoon or two, and will not make any difference to your cooking results.

MEASURING EQUIPMENT

The difference between measuring cups internationally is minimal within 2 or 3 teaspoons' difference. (For the record, 1 Australian metric measuring cup will hold approximately 250ml.) The most accurate way of measuring dry ingredients is to weigh them. When measuring liquids use a clear glass or plastic jug with the metric markings.

If you would like the measuring cups and spoons as used in our Test Kitchen, turn to page 128 for details and order coupon. In this book we use metric measuring cups and spoons approved by Standards Australia.

● a graduated set of four cups for measuring dry ingredients; the sizes are marked on the cups.

● a graduated set of four spoons for measuring dry and liquid ingredients; the amounts are marked on the spoons.

● 1 TEASPOON: 5ml

● 1 TABLESPOON: 20ml.

NOTE: NZ, CANADA, USA AND UK ALL USE 15ml TABLESPOONS.
ALL CUP AND SPOON MEASUREMENTS ARE LEVEL.

DRY MEASURES

METRIC	IMPERIAL
15g	1/2oz
30g	1oz
60g	2oz
90g	3oz
125g	4oz (1/4lb)
155g	5oz
185g	6oz
220g	7oz
250g	8oz (1/2lb)
280g	9oz
315g	10oz
345g	11oz
375g	12oz (3/4lb)
410g	13oz
440g	14oz
470g	15oz
500g	16oz (1lb)
750g	24oz (11/2lb)
1kg	32oz (2lb)

LIQUID MEASURES

METRIC	IMPERIAL
30ml	1 fluid oz
60ml	2 fluid oz
100ml	3 fluid oz
125ml	4 fluid oz
150ml	5 fluid oz (1/4 pint/1 gill)
190ml	6 fluid oz
250ml	8 fluid oz
300ml	10 fluid oz (1/2 pint)
500ml	16 fluid oz
600ml	20 fluid oz (1 pint)
1000ml (1 litre)	13/4 pints

WE USE LARGE EGGS WITH AN AVERAGE WEIGHT OF 60g

HELPFUL MEASURES

METRIC	IMPERIAL
3mm	1/8in
6mm	1/4in
1cm	1/2in
2cm	3/4in
2.5cm	1in
5cm	2in
6cm	21/2in
8cm	3in
10cm	4in
13cm	5in
15cm	6in
18cm	7in
20cm	8in
23cm	9in
25cm	10in
28cm	11in
30cm	12in (1ft)

HOW TO MEASURE

When using the graduated metric measuring cups, it is important to shake the dry ingredients loosely into the required cup. Do not tap the cup on the bench, or pack the ingredients into the cup unless otherwise directed. Level top of cup with knife. When using graduated metric measuring spoons, level top of spoon with knife. When measuring liquids in the jug, place jug on flat surface, check for accuracy at eye level.

OVEN TEMPERATURES

These oven temperatures are only a guide; we've given you the lower degree of heat. Always check the manufacturer's manual.

	C° (Celsius)	F° (Fahrenheit)	Gas Mark
Very slow	120	250	1
Slow	150	300	2
Moderately slow	160	325	3
Moderate	180 - 190	350 - 375	4
Moderately hot	200 - 210	400 - 425	5
Hot	220 - 230	450 - 475	6
Very hot	240 - 250	500 - 525	7

TWO GREAT OFFERS FROM THE AWW HOME LIBRARY

Here's the perfect way to keep your Home Library books in order, clean and within easy reach. More than a dozen books fit into this smart silver grey vinyl folder. PRICE: Australia $11.95; elsewhere $21.95; prices include postage and handling. To order your holder, see the details below.

All recipes in the AWW Home Library are created using Australia's unique system of metric cups and spoons. While it is relatively easy for overseas readers to make any minor conversions required, it is easier still to own this durable set of Australian cups and spoons (photographed). PRICE : Australia: $5.95; New Zealand: $A8.00; elsewhere: $A9.95; prices include postage & handling.
This offer is available in all countries.

TO ORDER YOUR METRIC MEASURING SET OR BOOK HOLDER:

PHONE: Have your credit card details ready. Sydney: (02) 9260 0035; **elsewhere in Australia:** 1800 252 515 (free call, Mon-Fri, 9am-5pm) or FAX your order to (02) 9267 4363 or MAIL your order by photocopying or cutting out and completing the coupon below.

PAYMENT: **Australian residents:** We accept the credit cards listed, money orders and cheques. **Overseas residents:** We accept the credit cards listed, drafts in $A drawn on an Australian bank, also English, New Zealand and U.S. cheques in the currency of the country of issue.
Credit card charges are at the exchange rate current at the time of payment.

Please photocopy and complete coupon and fax or send to:
AWW Home Library Reader Offer, ACP Direct, PO Box 7036, Sydney 1028.

❏ Metric Measuring Set ❏ Holder

Please indicate number(s) required.

Mr/Mrs/Ms _____

Address_____

_____

Postcode _____ Country_____

Ph: ( ) _____Bus. Hour: _____

I enclose my cheque/money order for $ _____ payable to ACP Direct

OR: please charge my:

❏ Bankcard ❏ Visa ❏ MasterCard ❏ Diners Club ❏ Amex

☐☐☐☐☐☐☐☐☐☐☐☐☐☐☐☐☐ Exp. Date ___/__

Cardholder's signature _____

(Please allow up to 30 days for delivery within Australia. Allow up to 6 weeks for overseas deliveries.)

Both offers expire 30/6/97.   AWSF97